THE CONSTITUTIONAL BALANCE

In *The Constitutional Balance* Sir John Laws has left a vivid and timely commentary on one of the most pressing issues in the legal world today.

The debate continues whether or not judges venture too far into issues of Government policy, and whether or not there are any limits on the power of the executive and the legislature to propose and enact legislation that unduly restricts fundamental freedoms in a democratic society subject to the rule of law.

Sir John Laws examines the relationship between constitutional fundamentals and values. He finds basic ideals of reason, fairness and the presumption of liberty in the common law, and recognises that a democratically accountable executive and legislature must be able to make policy and enact and implement legislation to pursue social goals. The courts then interpret the laws. As Sir John puts it – "The meeting of Parliament and the common law, in the crucible of statutory interpretation, is close to the core of [the constitutional balance]".

These fundamental values can compete with each other, giving rise to tensions within and between key state institutions, in particular the executive and the judiciary. A 'constitutional balance' between them must be found if the constitution is to function properly, each institution is to understand the proper extent and limits of its authority, and the rule of law is to be maintained. Sir John draws on his life-long experience as a barrister, judge and academic, and on case-law and learning, to explain in vibrant and engaging terms how such a 'constitutional balance' might be achieved.

The Constitutional Balance

John Laws

·HART·

OXFORD · LONDON · NEW YORK · NEW DELHI · SYDNEY

HART PUBLISHING

Bloomsbury Publishing Plc

Kemp House, Chawley Park, Cumnor Hill, Oxford, OX2 9PH, UK

1385 Broadway, New York, NY 10018, USA

29 Earlsfort Terrace, Dublin 2, Ireland

HART PUBLISHING, the Hart/Stag logo, BLOOMSBURY and the Diana logo are
trademarks of Bloomsbury Publishing Plc

First published in Great Britain 2021

A catalogue record for this book is available from the British Library.

Library of Congress Cataloging-in-Publication data

Names: Laws, John, 1945–2020, author.

Title: The constitutional balance / John Laws.

Description: Oxford, UK ; New York, NY : Hart Publishing, an imprint of Bloomsbury Publishing, 2021. |
Includes bibliographical references and index.

Identifiers: LCCN 2020040408 (print) | LCCN 2020040409 (ebook) |
ISBN 9781509935451 (hardback) | ISBN 9781509935468 (Epub) | ISBN 9781509935475 (pdf)

Subjects: LCSH: Constitutional law. | Civil rights. | Fairness. | Liberty. | Parliamentary practice.

Classification: LCC K3165 .L39 2020 (print) | LCC K3165 (ebook) | DDC 342/.001—dc23

LC record available at https://lccn.loc.gov/2020040408

LC ebook record available at https://lccn.loc.gov/2020040409

ISBN: HB: 978-1-50993-545-1
       ePDF: 978-1-50993-547-5
       ePub: 978-1-50993-546-8

Typeset by Compuscript Ltd, Shannon

To find out more about our authors and books visit www.hartpublishing.co.uk. Here you will find
extracts, author information, details of forthcoming events and the option to sign up for our newsletters.

Photo: Garlinda Birkbeck

In Memoriam

The Right Honourable Sir John Laws
Sometime Lord Justice of Appeal
1945–2020

Jurist, scholar and friend
Husband, father and grandfather
Requiescat in pace

In 1984, aged three, I declared I didn't want to be a 'boring barrister like Daddy when I grow up'. Although I was correct in that I didn't follow in my father's footsteps with a legal career, my description of him as boring was nothing short of toddler irascibility. Rather, he was electric: unbelievably clever, hilariously funny and wonderfully kind with a love of eccentric jumpers and ties.

He had the most amazing way with words, which would captivate anyone. From an early age, he would tell me epic stories then quiz me afterwards about the characters' choices and foibles. He relished his role as a devoted grandfather to my children, James and Sophie.

He gave me a strong moral compass to champion the greater good; an ability to look for holes in any argument, and a love of Greece and cats.

Happily married for 44 years, he and my mother Sophie were the original power couple: incredibly bright, charming and loved by everyone they met all over the world. Sadly, after she died in June 2017, he lost his joie de vivre but his natural wit continued to the end in April 2020, charming all of his medical and care teams.

His coat of arms created for his year as Treasurer of The Inner Temple in 2010 perfectly captured him. Featuring an Attic owl, Edward Lear's pussy-cat, a devil, and the epigrammatic motto 'leges honorandae' (the laws must be obeyed), my father was the true antithesis of boring, and his wonderful legacy will continue.

Margaret Grace Laws
December 2020

FOREWORD

Long after almost all his contemporaries are forgotten, Sir John Laws will be remembered and appreciated as a man who was a brilliant and principled legal thinker, above all on constitutional and public law issues, and who made his points in beautiful and punchy language. One only has to dip into this book to appreciate the importance of the issues he addressed and the extraordinarily high quality both of his intellect and of his powers of expression. Many of the ideas in this book originate from John's magisterial judgments and sparkling speeches, which are a joy to read. However, reading past judgments and speeches is something of a minority pastime, and anyway, like all great thinkers, his ideas developed over the years.

Sir John therefore had the typically inspired idea, which was also an indication of his commitment to the topic, that, on his retirement from the bench, he should write a short and accessible book setting out the culmination of his thoughts and reflections on the UK's constitution. Very sadly, he fell ill and died before he could finish the book, and Nigel Pleming QC, together with the publishers, took over the final editing, initially in collaboration with Sir John. Anyone interested in or concerned about our constitution owes a great debt to Mr Pleming and the publishers for bringing this book to a wider public.

Professor David Feldman QC, with some input from Mr Pleming, has also written an excellent Preface to this book summarising its origins and subject-matter, and the influence Sir John's thinking has had. It would therefore be otiose for me to say anything further in this brief Foreword about this book, other than to welcome it very warmly and to commend it whole-heartedly, not just to lawyers and philosophers, but also to everyone with any interest in that most elusive and fascinating of topics, the UK constitution.

I would, however, like to write a few words about John Laws more personally. To those of us who had the privilege of being his judicial colleagues, he was a memorably stimulating, always generous companion, both in and out of court. In court, he treated all advocates and litigants, and indeed his judicial colleagues, with courtesy, and he was never rude. When he was being addressed by an obtuse counsel, John was tolerant, but did not waste time. He always made his points to counsel in court and to his colleagues in discussions outside court in clear terms, but he was never aggressive. Indeed, he positively relished being contradicted, as there was nothing he liked better than an intellectual argument, which he always conducted with good humour and total lack of rancour.

As any reader of this book will quickly appreciate, John was a man of high principles, to which he adhered rigorously. However, he was very far indeed from being a prig. Socially, he treated everyone he talked to as his equal, and loved intellectually challenging discussions, but was also happy to indulge in small talk. He genuinely cared about people, and is fondly and gratefully remembered by many former law students and pupils for the genuine interest he showed in them, and the practical support he gave them.

John was a somewhat roly-poly figure, with thick floppy hair and twinkling eyes behind thickly lensed spectacles, through which he looked at you with a penetrating gaze. He had a taste for arresting ties and socks, and a love of ancient and modern Greece and a fondness for cats. Whether one met him at a social or a professional event, it did not take long to appreciate his unusual combination of intellectual acuity, verbal fluency, moral probity and personal benevolence, spiced with a mild, but unmistakable and endearing dose of eccentricity. All these qualities have come together in this book.

David Neuberger
November 2020

PREFACE

I. The Origins of this Book

The book encapsulates Sir John Laws's final reflections on the United Kingdom's constitution after nearly 40 years of intensive immersion in public law as barrister, judge, lecturer and author. He was encouraged to bring his thoughts together when the University of Cambridge elected him to be the AL Goodhart Visiting Professor of Legal Science for 2016–17, following his retirement from the Court of Appeal in 2016 at the age of 71. He and Sophie, his wife and soul-mate of over 40 years, revelled in the collegial spirit and lively intellectual and social environment of the Faculty of Law and of Robinson College (of which he was an Honorary Fellow). He threw himself wholeheartedly into the life of the Cambridge Law Faculty. Given the chance to deliver a course of lectures on a subject of his choice, he settled on 'Judicial Review and the Constitution', allowing him to take stock of a field to which he had made seminal contributions, bringing to bear his varied experiences as a student of classics and ancient history, barrister, including eight years as First Junior Treasury Counsel (Common Law) or 'Treasury Devil', advising government on a very wide range of public law matters and representing them in court, and 24 years as a judge of the High Court and Court of Appeal of England and Wales.

More than any other judge of his generation, Sir John developed English public law by applying a value-based theory of the constitution, especially of the proper relationships between citizens and their institutions of government and between those institutions among themselves, paying particular attention to the relationship between political and judicial institutions in a representative democracy. Through much of his career Sir John argued for his politico-legal philosophy extra-judicially, in articles, lectures and books.[1] While his core values remained consistent, he refined his ideas. As Goodhart Professor he prepared, with utmost care, 14 lectures, and delivered them with his customarily engaging bonhomie tempered by slightly surprising trepidation. His last months in Cambridge were overshadowed when Sophie was found to be suffering from untreatable cancer, from which she died in June 2017. Sir John's lectures were compelling, constituting a carefully considered restatement of his thinking about fundamentals of the United Kingdom's constitution.

---

[1] His main relevant publications are listed at the end of this Preface.

He subsequently decided to convert the lectures into a book. Unfortunately his own health declined. He was able to complete the text, but by reason of his own physical incapacity required the assistance of others, including that of his friend and former colleague Nigel Pleming QC, to tidy the manuscript, track down references, liaise with his publisher and, with the full support of Sir John's daughter, Margaret Grace, to ensure that his book would be published, albeit post-humously. The pages that follow are, nevertheless, entirely Sir John's own thoughts, arguments and insights in his own words and distinctive style.

In the transition from 14 lectures to an Introduction and nine chapters, Sir John introduced some new material and rearranged the structure. In his lectures, Sir John began with an introduction, followed it with two lectures on the Rule of Law and the common law's distinctive contribution to it, then three lectures on the role of judicial review in maintaining and enhancing the Rule of Law. Lectures seven and eight were on the constitutional basis of judicial review. Then came a lecture on the idea of democracy, and one on what he called the 'two moralities' of politics and the judiciary respectively. Lectures 11 to 14 discussed whether democracy and judicial review were conflicting values, focusing particularly on the idea of judicial deference in the context of adjudication about human rights.

For the book, he placed fundamental concepts front and centre, including ideology (Introduction), the Rule of Law (chapter 1), democracy (chapter 2) and the 'two moralities', with an introduction to techniques of mediating between them (chapter 3). There follows a discussion of the common law and its constitutional position in relation to statute, including techniques of statutory interpretation (chapter 4), and of the fundamental common law constitutional values of reason, fairness and the presumption of liberty (chapter 5). Having established the judiciary's constitutional role, chapter 6 picks up from chapter 3 the task of 'finding the edge' that divides the constitutional space properly occupied by the political arms of government and the judiciary, using the technique of 'judicial deference'. In chapter 7, Sir John explored different theories about the factors that underpin judicial review of executive action, rejecting the idea of parliamentary intent and what has come to be known as the 'ultra vires doctrine',[2] and in chapter 8 he considered the implications for the important constitutional doctrine of parliamentary sovereignty.

Having established his notion of 'constitutional balance' and explored its implications from a variety of angles, he devoted chapter 9 to a number of threats to that balance, especially those stemming from the ways judges have applied the Human Rights Act 1998, and threats to freedom of thought, belief and

---

[2] A position adopted by Sir John in 'Illegality: the Problem of Jurisdiction' in Supperstone & Goudie (eds), *Judicial Review* (Butterworth, 1992), written at about the time of Sir John's 'transition from Junior Treasury Counsel to High Court judge'; Lord Carnwath in *R (Privacy International) v Investigatory Powers Tribunal* [2019] UKSC 22, [2020] AC 491 [81].

expression, including that from religious zealotry. He returned to the danger of ideology and the importance of the fundamental values of reason, fairness and presumption of liberty, and brought back to the spotlight judicial independence and 'deference', which he thought threatened the constitutional balance when British judges simply accept, as if binding on them, judgments of the European Court of Human Rights not subject to the constitutional constraints he considered that the United Kingdom's balanced constitution imposes on her judiciary.

II. The Idea of 'Constitutional Balance'

At the heart of the book lies a classic conundrum in democratic thought. Democrats locate ultimate political authority in 'the people' as a whole, and give their representatives ultimate power to make and change laws and policies to advance public welfare. Democracy depends on freedoms, especially of thought and expression, yet democratically legitimated rules and policies often restrict them in pursuit of collective goals. How can the risk of undermining the conditions for democratic politics best be managed? Sir John advanced a complex answer: different institutions take primary responsibility for defending freedom and for protecting welfare, and check each other's excesses by respectfully reflecting, in their decision-making, on the strengths and weaknesses of their own moral claims to authority. Politicians principally pursue social goals; judges principally protect individuals' liberties.

This emphasis on the judges' role in protecting liberty is both normative and descriptive. It reflects Sir John's beliefs in the close relationship between people's responsibility for their actions and their liberty, and in the power of reason to aid good decision-making by individuals and governments. He believed in individuals' capacity to make morally good choices, and held that they should have the freedom necessary to decide how to choose their paths even if their choices were (others might say) bad or wrong. Without that freedom it would be immoral to hold them responsible for their actions. He opposed ideology, which he defined in the Introduction to this book as 'a preconception or preconceptions, an assumption or assumptions, not tested by reason, by argument, by practice or by results; an *a priori* belief, given or imposed in advance, assumed to be true'. Ideologies exclude reason and rational argument, and try to force people to surrender their own freedom of thought and expression. Freedoms must be limited to some extent, however, by the needs of society. State institutions are responsible for advancing social welfare and setting appropriate standards for that purpose, but those responsibilities must, under the United Kingdom's constitution, be discharged for the public benefit, and political institutions have to be democratically accountable. As an ancient historian and philosopher (subjects he studied as an undergraduate, which became part of his system of thought), he saw both the strengths and dangers of democracy, which can be as prone as autocracies to adopt ideologies.

A major theme is that freedom flourishes only in the absence of ideology, and that a good constitution must therefore find a balance between democracy and freedom that does not foreclose argument or exclude reason.

Such is the 'constitutional balance' of which Sir John writes, between competing constitutional values, and between two sets of institutions motivated primarily by different types of values and two distinct moralities. The inevitable and proper tension between them could destroy the state if allowed to become excessively confrontational. People in each institution had, therefore, to understand and accommodate each other's responsibilities and needs as much as possible in order to keep the state operating effectively and fairly, recognising that each institution pursued the welfare of the people, albeit in different ways.[3]

Sir John was both liberal and a democrat. He went out of his way to make it clear that, in his view, politics and politicians worked, and rightly worked, according to a different morality from that of courts. Giving appropriate weight to the 'two moralities' was at the heart of his conception of the balanced constitution. Political morality was largely forward-looking, utilitarian and collective: legislators and Ministers had necessarily to plan for the good of the community as a whole, and could legitimately pursue that end by making policies and laws designed to produce beneficial, social effects. Judicial morality, by contrast, Sir John saw as concentrating principally on particular disputes regarding individuals' obligations and freedoms. Judges justify their decisions by seeking rules, principles and answers in a long tradition of judicial decision-making carried forward through enacted laws and earlier judgments. Where they develop the law, they do so gradually, by principled interpretation of legislation and by analogy with previously accepted principles and remedies. By the nature of the judicial process, judges can only rarely take account of collective social goals (unless giving effect to legislation designed to advance them). Instead, for hundreds of years, common-law judges have sought to give life to the fundamental values of reason, fairness and a presumption in favour of individuals' liberty.

Judicial review of administrative and executive action was constitutionally required because these fundamental constitutional values of reason, fairness and the presumption of liberty demanded of judges 'a continuing and evolving determination to call decision-makers to an adherence to standards of integrity and reason'.[4] It protected people against infringement of their liberties through abuse of powers granted by Parliament. Sir John therefore rejected the idea known as 'ultra vires theory', according to which judges are authorised to scrutinise executive action only because Parliament has impliedly permitted such review by not legislating to prevent it, or by legislating within a matrix of constitutional values with

---

[3] The design for the front cover of this book, selected by Sir John's daughter Margaret Grace, is inspired by this: the Greek goddess Dike, who represented justice, moral order and judgment according to socially enforced customary rules, operated alongside Eunomia, goddess of law and legislation, government according to law, and so captured the essence of the 'two moralities' at the heart of Sir John's balanced constitution.

[4] J Laws, 'Judicial Review: the ghost in the machine: principle in public law' [1989] *PL* 27, 31.

which judicial review is in harmony.[5] Sir John considered that his model entailed judicial protection for fundamental, constitutional, common law rights that the legislature and executive ought not to infringe without very strong, reasoned justification. The judges, usually not the legislature, identify these rights, which take the form of negative liberties, not positive rights. That is to say, they were rights to be free from interference, not rights to receive benefits from society. The latter, which we can call welfare rights, were not constitutionally fundamental because they depended on a positive decision by the legislature to award them, and were properly subject to political debate. Negative freedoms, such as freedom of expression and freedom of thought, were properly in the keeping of courts, because they did not need to be granted by legislation; in fact legislation was more likely to limit than increase the total set of liberties available to people, in pursuit of collective goods. Fundamental liberties were not constitutive of State institutions (although Sir John argued that the legitimacy of the State's institutions and officials depended in part on the degree to which they respected people's liberties). Instead, they were the subject of constitutional obligations binding all institutions, but the judiciary particularly, to protect them, compatibly with other constitutional requirements such as the sovereignty of Parliament.

How were courts to defend fundamental rights against legislation appearing to restrict them? First, judges would so far as possible interpret legislation so as not to restrict liberties, or not restrict them more than necessary. By relying principally on interpretation, a well-established judicial responsibility, rather than letting judges refuse to apply legislation violating fundamental liberties, Sir John retained parliamentary sovereignty, at least in form. He did not say, expressly, that judges need not apply fundamentally unconstitutional legislation, which Lord Carnwath JSC has contemplated.[6] However, in chapter 8[7] he considered the dilemma, 'What if Parliament were to abridge or even overthrow our constitutional principles?' His response was not to suggest a hard-edged limitation on the power of Parliament to legislate, or the imposition of a higher power that would entitle the judges to quash, or strike down, such legislation. But he did at least contemplate a position where legislation was 'so outrageous that any conscientious judge would think it contrary to his or her judicial oath to uphold it'.

Sir John did not see the working constitution as a simple hierarchy of abstract constitutional rules. His model was both more nuanced and more political. Nuances included treating some 'constitutional' legislation as being protected against implied repeal by later legislation.[8] The political character lay in his view of

---

[5] A number of significant contributions to this debate, which continues today, are collected in C Forsyth (ed), *Judicial Review and the Constitution* (Hart Publishing, 2000). See further ch 7 of this book.

[6] *R (Privacy International) v Investigatory Powers Tribunal* [2019] UKSC 22, [2020] AC 491 [144].

[7] Ch 8, section II.

[8] *Thoburn v Sunderland City Council* [2002] EWHC 195 (Admin), [2003] QB 151, DC, some of the implications being discussed in *R (Buckinghamshire County Council) v Secretary of State for Transport* [2014] UKSC 3, [2014] 1 WLR 324, SC.

the constitution as a practical process of exploration and accommodation between institutions with different but equally important responsibilities and sources of authority. Like Lord Bridge and Sir Stephen Sedley, he saw the constitution as resting on twin foundations; Parliament and courts were each sovereign in their own spheres and functions, the executive being subject to both.[9]

Another way in which fundamental constitutional liberties were to be protected was by judges' requiring officials to give good reasons for actions and decisions adversely affecting liberties, and rejecting the reasons if they were unreasonable. Fundamental liberties were thus not inviolable but required justification that met the test of reason. One of Sir John's favourite legal texts was the classic statement by Lord Greene MR in *Associated Provincial Picture Houses Ltd v Wednesbury Corporation*,[10] of the various ways in which courts may, and may not, scrutinise the reasonableness of executive decision-making.

All parts of these arguments were controversial. In a critique of Sir John's ideas up to 1999,[11] Professor John Griffith pointed out that the special position of negative liberties in Sir John's constitution, necessary as it is for political liberals and philosophical Kantians, could not be accepted by non-liberals. Griffith saw no reason to treat individuals' liberties as more important than general welfare: 'I would willingly see some negative rights denied on occasion to the rich and powerful if the consequences were that more positive benefits accrued to the less fortunate.'[12] Removing important decisions from democratic processes into courts was liable to lead to totalitarianism.[13] Liberties were always more valuable to people who can use them most fully, and those were generally relatively well-off people who tend to have social or political influence and therefore rely less on courts to protect their interests. People who were less well-off and had less access to social and political influence to protect their interests were particularly likely to need protection from courts, but were also least likely to be able to afford to invoke it. A constitution that systematically privileged the rights of the well-off over the rights of the socially marginalised would not be one with which anyone other than a liberal Kantian was likely to feel comfortable. Griffith also questioned whether, in a democracy, one ought to rely on judges to identify the interests that are to receive special protection, both because judges tend to be drawn from backgrounds that limit their experience of the least well-off in society and because they are not constitutionally accountable for their decisions.

It is clear that liberal political philosophy underpins Sir John's position, and those who do not share that philosophy are unlikely to regard as persuasive his

---

[9] *X v Morgan Grampian Ltd* [1991] AC 1, 48 *per* Lord Bridge; Sir Stephen Sedley, 'The common law and the constitution' in Lord Nolan and Sir Stephen Sedley, *The Making & Remaking of the British Constitution* (Blackstone Press, 1997) 25, 26.

[10] *Associated Provincial Picture Houses Ltd v Wednesbury Corporation* [1948] 1 KB 223, CA.

[11] JAG Griffith, 'The brave new world of Sir John Laws' (2000) 63 *MLR* 159.

[12] ibid 172.

[13] ibid 176, following Lord Devlin, *The Judge* (Oxford University Press, 1979) 17.

argument that protecting liberty and reason against executive action is, in a democracy, a normatively satisfactory justification for judicial review. But Sir John argued that fundamental liberties, reason and fairness were not values chosen *a priori* as worthy of constitutional status and judicial protection, but had been embedded for centuries at the moral heart of the common law tradition. It was, he thought, the distinctive genius of the common law to provide a method of reasoning that rigorously tested rules and interpretation in the context of concrete cases, prioritised consistency, yet allowed room for experimenting with new concepts or developments where existing authorities seemed inadequate for the needs of a particular case. The mixture of principled consistency, rigorous analysis and experimentation by reinterpretation and analogy produced law that was tough and durable, because it had been argued over by lawyers and judges examining different factual situations and ethical demands, producing consistent fundamental values. Common law develops not in a series of new starts but as a connected chain. Judges developing it would be adding a new link, which must remain faithful to the design of the earlier links. Professor Ronald Dworkin wrote that judges are authors as well as interpreters of the law, their authorship being best understood through the metaphor of a 'chain novel': each author successively contributes to the legal matrix as consistently as possible with the character and plot-lines in previous chapters.[14] Sir John took a similar view, putting legal tradition at the heart of common law creativity. Legislation, by contrast, is sudden, not reliant on tradition, and is not required to adopt consistent values over time. It is fundamental to representative democracy that legislative changes are unconstrained by the past (except so far as some changes required attention to be given to problems they might cause for existing rules and procedures). The idea that Parliament cannot bind its successors is central to parliamentary sovereignty.[15]

This is the special strength of legislation, but it also means that legislation is temporary, as today's statute can just as easily be repealed tomorrow.

III. Managing the Constitution's Inherent Tensions

Recognising that judges and politicians must quite legitimately march to different tunes with different forms of discipline and justification presented Sir John with a problem. What happens when these two different moralities and methods conflict? How should a judge resolve a case that pits a public body seeking to implement legislation that pursues a policy intended for social improvement against an individual seeking to protect a personal interest against an alleged abuse of power? If judges were to ignore the legitimacy of public bodies' utilitarian morality and

---

[14] R Dworkin, *Law's Empire* (Fontana, 1986) 228–32.
[15] See, eg, AV Dicey, *Lectures Introductory to the Study of the Law of the Constitution*, 1st edn (Macmillan, 1885), Lecture II, esp at 60–64.

executive methods, or politicians and administrators were to ignore the legitimacy of judicial morality, irreducible dislocation would follow between key institutions. Executives cannot achieve much without legal, and in the last resort judicial, support; judges cannot discharge their responsibility to give fair hearings in individual cases unless the executive provides them with necessary resources (a problem at the time of writing) and abides by and respects judges' decisions. Sir John saw a growing danger of such a dislocation in the first two decades of the twenty-first century, exacerbated but not caused by fractious disputes related to the United Kingdom's withdrawal from the European Union. Good sense and understanding would be needed from each institution to maintain the effectiveness and authority of laws, including those made by Parliament, and the authority and effectiveness of courts. Both were necessary if the constitution of the United Kingdom was to continue to reflect the democratic legitimacy given expression in parliamentary sovereignty and the judicial role necessary for parliamentary sovereignty to be effective and also for maintaining the rule of law (itself a contentious term). Indeed, he argued that the legislative sovereignty of Parliament entailed a requirement for an independent judiciary, not because Parliament had tacitly authorised it but because statutes could not be effective unless some independent person or body – independent of Parliament and of the executive – had ultimate authority to decide what statutes meant. Without it, the meaning of statutory provisions would be 'degraded to nothing more than a matter of opinion',[16] and statutes would not provide a reasonably clear guide to people's legal obligations. On this view, attempts by Parliament to exclude judicial oversight of the lawfulness of executive decision-making should be resisted so as to protect effective parliamentary sovereignty.

Mutual respect between political and judicial institutions is not easy to achieve and can easily be eroded. The rule of law requires self-discipline on the part of legislators and Ministers, who must accept (sometimes to their frustration) that respect for legal interests and principles may limit their freedom of action. Professor Sir Jeffrey Jowell has called it an 'institutional morality',[17] a commitment treated as binding by all who are concerned with government. Courts consider themselves to have a particularly strong role in ensuring that parties to litigation have complied

---

[16] *R (Cart) v Upper Tribunal* [2009] EWHC 3052 (Admin), [2011] Q.B. 120 [38]. Sir John's statement of principle in *Cart* was approved by the Supreme Court in *R (Privacy International) v Investigatory Powers Tribunal* [2019] UKSC 22, [2019] 2 WLR 1219, a case in which the majority gave a very restricted interpretation to a clause that appeared to exclude judicial review of the Tribunal, in judgments of both majority and dissenting Justices: see [160] *per* Lord Lloyd-Jones, [190] *per* Lord Sumption (with whom Lord Reed agreed), dissenting, and [236] *per* Lord Wilson, dissenting. Lord Carnwath (with whom Lady Hale and Lord Kerr agreed) in the majority delivered a judgment that was at least not inconsistent with Sir John's statement of principle. In *Cart*, in the Supreme Court ([2011] UKSC 28, [2012] 1AC 663), Lady Hale said '[t]he rule of law requires that statute law be interpreted by an authoritative and independent judicial source' (ibid [30]), expressly approving other parts of para [38] of Sir John's judgment.
[17] J Jowell, 'The Rule of Law' in J Jowell, D Oliver and C O'Cinneide (eds), *The Changing Constitution*, 9th edn (Oxford University Press, 2019) ch 1, 17.

with the law, the whole of the law, not limited to statutes and subordinate legislation. But in doing so, judges should, Sir John thought, recognise that public bodies may properly have many reasons for exercising discretion in a particular way, and may be better placed than judges (for reasons of expertise, access to the best sources of information on a subject, or their democratic accountability) to make assessments on some contested issues.

Sir John encapsulated this in a notion of 'deference': judges, he thought, should give great weight to the views and reasons of experts and politicians on some matters.[18] He expressed this most clearly in his dissenting judgment in *International Transport Roth GmbH v Secretary of State for the Home Department*,[19] a case concerning a very large fixed penalty imposed on carriers and their drivers for having been used unknowingly by clandestine entrants to the United Kingdom. Courts generally exercise a supervisory role in relation to administrative decision-making: Ministers or administrators make the initial, substantive decision; the court's role is to ensure that it was made lawfully. This may require judges to evaluate decisions on a number of grounds. For example, in deciding whether the penalty scheme in *International Transport Roth* was consistent with common law values of reasonableness and fairness and with human rights given effect through the Human Rights Act 1998, a question concerning the legality of interfering with a protected right might require a court to decide whether the interference was proportionate with the right so as to be 'necessary in a democratic society' for a permitted purpose. When making that decision, courts should, Sir John thought, show greater 'deference' to assessments enshrined in an Act of Parliament than to those made by the executive, although the latter too would be entitled to some degree of 'deference' on democratic grounds; more deference when the Convention right in terms requires a balance to be struck than when it is expressed in unqualified terms; more 'deference' to the political arm where the matter is specially within their area of constitutional responsibility than otherwise, of which primary examples are defence and macro-economic policy. Finally, greater 'deference' was to be paid when an issue was within the expertise of democratically accountable institutions than when it was within an area of particular judicial expertise.

The notion of 'deference' can perhaps be seen as a response to some of Griffith's criticisms, mentioned in section II of this Preface. It was an attempt to show that judges could give weight to collective interests in a principled way. In his dissenting judgment in *International Transport Roth*, he gave perhaps excessive weight to

---

[18] Some judges have subsequently distanced themselves from the word 'deference', but the idea underlying it remains, and Sir John retained the term in this book. See the discussions in chs 3 and 6. In ch 9, section I.D, Sir John uses the word in the context of Convention rights: 'There would be no denial of the Convention rights in a decision of our courts that respects the constitutional balance, and which therefore give a degree – perhaps a decisive degree – of deference to the elected powers' view of the public interest.'

[19] *International Transport Roth GmbH v Secretary of State for the Home Department* [2002] EWCA Civ 158, [2003] QB 728 [83]–[87].

the executive's view. Had his assessment prevailed, the court would have upheld a scheme that, as a whole, Simon Brown LJ considered 'quite frankly unfair'. Jonathan Parker LJ called it 'a disproportionate and unjustified inroad into the carrier's right of silence and hence into the presumption of innocence which is expressly safeguarded by Article 6(2)' of the Convention, 'wholly unfair' to who would be liable even if they knew nothing of the presence of illegal entrants on their vehicles, and lacking a suitably expeditious method for deciding whether the vehicles themselves should be detained and for how long. The whole scheme disproportionately interfered with the right to a fair hearing and the right to property.[20] Sir John was prepared to allow far more leeway to the executive than fellow judges were, and would have exercised the judges' supervisory role with a very light touch indeed.

This highlights a problem with 'deference': if treated as a constitutional obligation of judges, it risks making judicial protection for individuals' Convention rights against the executive hollow, and the rights themselves ineffective. It is the converse problem to that Griffith identified in Sir John's earlier writings, giving too much weight to individual liberty and not enough to collective interests. One might have expected Sir John to think that the duty to give a fair hearing lay squarely within the special expertise of courts rather than politicians. Taken too far, 'deference' threatens the moral authority of judges and the legal order.

If 'deference' is limited to questions of fact and evaluation, and encourages courts to respect (though not unquestioningly) findings and assessments made by people who have special expertise, 'deference' is perfectly acceptable. If it asks judges not to interfere in a cavalier way with judgments about defence, national security and macro-economic policy, by reason of the separation of powers and the political accountability of the executive or House of Commons, it is constitutionally unobjectionable. But when taken to the point where a court will not say, in respect of the right to a fair hearing, that a procedure as a whole is unfair and unjustified (fair hearings being part and parcel of what judges are appointed to give) because the executive has judged it to be desirable, it suggests that Sir John's enthusiasm for his developing argument could sometimes blind him to its proper limitations. Nevertheless, 'deference' usefully concentrated attention on the separation of powers, illuminated the fundamental difference between judicial and political roles and systems for justification, and attempted to systematise the process of 'finding the edge' in his balanced constitution.

It is a tragic consequence of Sir John's early death that this Preface is written without the benefit of discussion with the author, as to his reason for referring to 'deference' in the text, and on many other arguments in *The Constitutional Balance*. In chapter 8 (see section I) there is a passing reference to points in the text that will 'enliven future debate'. Those who were fortunate enough to listen to the lectures, or witness the annual debates between Sir John (as chair), David Feldman and

---

[20] ibid [47], [182], [183], [185], [193].

Paul Craig (as speakers), will have not the slightest doubt that the future debate would have been lively.

It is also to be regretted that Sir John is not with us to engage in, and contribute to, the current discussion over the limits of judicial review.[21] He would, we expect, have been a staunch defender of the *status quo* – there is an indicator of his position in chapter 8, section III, where he writes that 'the constitutional balance and our fundamental principles are particularly vulnerable to assaults, not least on the political front', quoting David Howarth, which extract we readily here repeat:

> [W]e should not be surprised to find that politicians interpret public law as essentially a political intervention by lawyers into politics and lawyers interpret it as a principled challenge to the lawlessness of politicians.

IV. Sir John's Intellectual Legacy

It is unusual to be able to trace an explicit and developing political and moral philosophy through a judge's judgments and extra-judicial writing. Sir John, philosopher as well as lawyer, engaged openly with philosophical questions affecting his constitutional ideas. This made him a target for criticism from people with different moral and political positions, but also made him publicly accountable for his views and decisions in a way that few judges can be. It earned him the respect of one of his most trenchant critics: as the era of the Human Rights Act 1998 dawned, John Griffith noted, 'at least we have some evidence to suggest how one Lord Justice of Appeal will consider the legal, political and philosophical problems. And for this we should be grateful.'[22] Sir John was never appointed to the Supreme Court, so we shall never know what influential judgments he might have delivered there with the benefit of discussion with colleagues.[23] He provided enough fresh insights to make us regret having missed those he might have offered from an even more elevated judicial position.

As this book shows, Sir John reminded us of the importance and contestability of law, its historical continuity and change, and the philosophical issues just beneath its surface, and he gave us a way of understanding the constitution that gives full value to the differences and tensions between, and modes of justification for, the moralities and roles of the state's various institutions. He offered philosophical clarity and realism while stressing the importance of principles.

---

[21] At the time of writing this Preface, an Independent Panel has been appointed to review judicial review and report to the Secretary of State for Justice, who will consider whether to propose reforms. The consultation can be accessed at www.gov.uk/government/groups/independent-review-of-administrative-law.

[22] Griffith, 'The brave new world of Sir John Laws' (n 11) 176.

[23] Sir John is described by Lord Brown as 'one of the finest jurists never to reach the final appeal court': Lord Brown, *Playing Off the Roof & Other Stories* (Marble Hill, 2020) 90.

We understand the constitution better, even if there are places in the analysis where we disagree with him. This is very important, especially when the constitution is as strongly contested as at present.

We hope, as Sir John would have hoped, that *The Constitutional Balance* stimulates debate, by fervent supporters, trenchant critics, by lawyers and politicians, by all interested in our constitution. He would have wanted nothing more.

David Feldman and Nigel Pleming

Sir John Laws' Main Relevant Publications

'Judicial Review: the ghost in the machine; principle in public law' [1989] *PL* 27

'Is the High Court the guardian of fundamental constitutional rights?' [1993] *PL* 59 (reprint of article in (1992) 18 *Commonwealth Law Bulletin* 1385)

'Illegality: the problem of jurisdiction' in M Supperstone and J Goudie (eds), *Judicial Review* (Butterworths, 1993) ch 4; extract from the second (1997) edition reproduced in C Forsyth (ed), *Judicial Review and the Constitution* (Hart Publishing, 2000) ch 4, 73

'Judicial remedies and the constitution' (1994) 57 *MLR* 213

'Law and democracy' [1995] *PL* 72

'The constitution: morals and rights' [1996] *PL* 622

'Public law and employment law: abuse of power' [1997] *PL* 455

'The limitations of human rights' [1998] *PL* 254

'Law and fact' [1999] *British Tax Review* 159

'Judicial review and the meaning of law' in C Forsyth (ed), *Judicial Review and the Constitution* (Hart Publishing, 2000) ch 8, 173

'Beyond rights' (2003) 23 *OJLS* 265

'Human rights and citizenship' (2004) 55 *Northern Ireland Legal Quarterly* 1

'A judicial perspective on the sacred in society' (2004) 6 *Ecclesiastical Law Journal* 317

'Review of Norman Doe (ed), *Portrayal of Religion: The Media and the Arts*' (2007) 9 *Ecclesiastical Law Journal* 229

With Carol Harlow, 'The rule of law: form or substance?' (2007) 4 *Justice Journal* 24

'Constitutional guarantees' (2008) 29 *Statute Law Review* 1

'Religion and law' (2011) 62 *South Carolina Law Review* 471

'Review of John Finnis, *Religion and Public Reason*' (2012) 14 *Ecclesiastical Law Journal* 299

'The good constitution' [2012] *CLJ* 567

'Sydney's sketches, Sydney's fingers – after dinner at the Inner Temple' (2014) 17 *Legal Ethics* 427

The Common Law Constitution (Cambridge University Press, 2014), the Hamlyn Lectures for 2013

In conversation with David Feldman at the Annual Conference of the Society for Legal Scholars, September 2014, available at https://sms.cam.ac.uk/media/1832294

'Review of Roger Trigg, *Religious Diversity: Philosophical and Political Dimensions*'(2016) 18 *Ecclesiastical Law Journal* 360

'The rule of law: the presumption of liberty and justice' (2017) 22 *Judicial Review* 365

'The *Miller* case and constitutional balance' in M Elliott, J Williams and AL Young (eds), *The UK Constitution after Miller* (Hart Publishing, 2018) ch 9, 203

The Balanced Constitution (Hart Publishing, 2020)

CONTENTS

Introduction*

'Democracy and the Rule of Law' is a mantra used time and again to summarise the virtues of the liberal State. We hear much less of the relationship *between* democracy and the Rule of Law. Plainly we need them both. Without the Rule of Law democratic government will swiftly be corrupted. Without democracy the Rule of Law is unlikely to survive long in the hands of an autocrat, though by great good fortune it has sometimes happened. Democracy's flag is the authority of the people's vote. Law's flag is more quartered: legal certainty, fairness and other qualities to which I shall come. They constrain the reach of democracy's power, and democracy's power seeks (often at least) to constrain the reach of law's principles. Hence the tension between the two. Its resolution is what I have called 'constitutional balance'.

The constitutional balance is the means by which our law gives practical application to constitutional principles that, as I shall argue in chapter 1, are (or should be treated as) the foundation of the Rule of Law. It has many facets and dimensions. It is very far from being no more than a tired and unappetising struggle for authority between the judges and the politicians; although it is coloured by an important distinction, between the respective moralities of the courts and government. The former is Kantian, the latter utilitarian. These two moralities are the subject of chapter 3.

A wise accommodation between the claims of the Rule of Law and the claims of democracy can only be struck on an anvil of principle. So we should ask: what are the principles that fuel the Rule of Law on the one hand and the rule of the popular vote on the other? The essence of the constitutional balance is to break down the separation between the two, so that the Rule of Law is inherent in democratic government and democratic government is inherent in the Rule of Law, at any rate in its practical application through the constitutional balance: see in particular chapter 2 (on democracy) and chapter 8 (on the sovereignty of Parliament). To make this good requires a wide canvas, and the themes of this book describe the contours of fundamental rights and freedoms: the constitutional pillars of reason, fairness and the presumption of liberty, and their relation to the Rule of Law; the virtue and vice of democracy; the contrasting moralities of law and politics; the dilemmas of legislative sovereignty and the fictitious notion (as I shall claim) of Parliamentary intent; the imperative of free thought and speech. The parts played

---

* This book has connections with my Hamlyn Lectures, published in 2014. See Sir John Laws, *The Common Law Constitution* (Cambridge University Press, 2014).

by all these elements in the workings of democratic government, their interplay with one another, will fashion the relationship between democracy and the Rule of Law, and thereby yield the constitutional balance.

I. The Vice of Ideology

But the fullness of the constitutional balance cannot be understood without reference to a prior theme, a seeming paradox. It is that the ideology of fundamental rights and freedoms is that there is no ideology. In his seminal essay *The Power of the Powerless*, Václav Havel, the Czech writer and statesman, said this:

> Ideology is a specious way of relating to the world. It offers human beings the illusion of an identity, of dignity, and of morality while making it easier for them to part with them.[1]

One may perhaps compare the comment of the Marquis de Vauvenargues in the eighteenth century, 'servitude debases men to the point where they end up liking it'.[2] There is also David Hume's observation, '[n]othing appears more surprising to those who consider human affairs with a philosophical eye, than the easiness with which the many are governed by the few'.[3]

Havel, of course, was speaking of ideology in the context of oppressive government. He considered that ideology furnished an 'illusion that the system [the system of government he so courageously opposed] is in harmony with the human order and the order of the universe'.[4] His striking observation, that ideology is a specious way of relating to the world, tells us something of what is required of a State that purports to secure constitutional rights for its citizens. It is that the constitution of such a State must be free of the hypnosis of ideologies of left and right, of religion and of atheism. I do not – of course – mean we must turn our backs on political and religious positions. We must turn our backs on the *hypnosis* of ideology, by which I mean what I take Havel to have meant: a preconception or preconceptions, an assumption or assumptions, not tested by reason, by argument, by practice or by results; an *a priori* belief, given or imposed in advance, assumed to be true.

Such blind ideologies are unfit as principles of conduct, whether for the State or the individual, for two reasons. The first objection is a logical one. The translation of such an ideology into a recipe for conduct very frequently rests on a command theory. Its putative veracity is dictated by the supposed command

---

[1] V Havel, 'The Power of the Powerless', tr P Wilson in V Havel et al, *The Power of the Powerless: Citizens Against the State in Central-Eastern Europe*, ed J Keane (Routledge, 1985) 23.
[2] Marquis de Vauvenargues, *Reflections and Maxims* (1746).
[3] D Hume, 'First Principles of Government', *Essays* (1742).
[4] Havel (n 1).

of someone else – God, or the dear leader, sometimes a long-dead dear leader. But the command theory is based on a fallacy. The fact that X commands you to do Y cannot of itself entail that you should do it. It is an instance of Hume's Law: you cannot derive an *ought* from an *is*.[5] The proposition that X commands you to do Y is a synthetic proposition, that is to say, a proposition of fact. No normative proposition can be deduced from it. The bare existence of a master's command, therefore, is of itself no basis whatever to require the servant's obedience. The master – X – cannot validly say, 'Obey me, because I am me.' There must always be a higher premise. The higher premise must consist in an established prior obligation to obey orders issued by X. But X cannot himself provide the higher premise. It is logically prior to him, and therefore must lie outside him. The logic is the same whether X is God or man.

Any attempt to formulate and justify the laws of the State wholly by reference to the command of a master, human or divine, denies this truth. It is therefore of the first importance that the command theory should be disavowed. It corrupts both democracy and the Rule of Law, and makes the constitutional balance impossible. No doubt, of course, a State may enact a law (or a person do an act) that reflects a command of the supposed master, where the reason for doing so is that the State or person independently judges it to be good; but that is quite a different matter.

The second objection to blind ideologies – to the command theory of moral or political conduct – marches closely with the first. It is that they are morally crippling. If you take your values entirely and uncritically from an external source, your own reason cannot moderate them; they are simply given to you. You cannot tailor your judgement in the light of experience; you cannot discard a failed principle in favour of something better, more humane. There is no scope for a self-correcting discipline. A doctrine, a belief system, arrived at uncritically as an act of actual or supposed obedience, is like a body with no immune system. It is a matter of chance, of luck, whether the master's command is bad or good. Think of the shame and inhumanity in exhorting murder for apostasy, or for that matter ostracism for homosexuality, simply because it says so in the Book.[6]

Here are two instances from religious contexts that exemplify the want of the higher premise and the abdication of the power to think for oneself, as Charles Freeman put it in *The Closing of the Western Mind*.[7] Freeman cites the words

---

[5] See D Hume, *Treatise of Human Nature*, III I (1739–40) 1. See also KR Popper, *The Open Society and Its Enemies*, vol I: *The Spell of Plato?* (Routledge, 2002) 50–53, and compare GE Moore's 'naturalistic fallacy': *Principia Ethica* (Cambridge University Press, 1903).

[6] A criticism by my grandfather, the Revd Professor JG McKenzie, of AJ Ayer's view of morality in *Language, Truth and Logic* (V Gollancz, 1936) contains a comparable idea: 'Ayer's statement that one of the "chief causes of moral behaviour is fear, both conscious and unconscious, of a god's displeasure, and fear of the enmity of society" is to reduce all morality to Super-ego morality, as a matter of fact to "borrowed morality" ... it is the free acceptance of a rational good which has led to our higher civilization' (JG McKenzie, *Guilt, Its Meaning and Significance* (first pub George Allen & Unwin Ltd, 1962; repub Routledge, 2016) 95).

[7] C Freeman, *The Closing of the Western Mind* (Pimlico, 2003) ch 16, 256.

of a Jesuit authority, quoted in William James' celebrated study, *The Varieties of Religious Experience*:

> One of the great consolations of the monastic life is the assurance we have that in obeying we can commit no fault. The Superior may commit a fault in commanding you to do this or that, but you are certain that you commit no fault so long as you obey, because God will only ask you if you have duly performed what orders you received, and if you can furnish a clear account in that respect, you are absolved entirely ... The moment what you did was done obediently, God wipes it out of your account and charges it to the Superior. So that Saint Jerome well exclaimed 'Oh, holy and blessed security by which one becomes almost impeccable'.[8]

The second instance concerns a Muslim's visit to the House of Commons, described by Bernard Lewis in *What Went Wrong? Western Impact and Middle Eastern Response*:

> In the first extant Muslim account of the British House of Commons, written by a visitor who went to England at the end of the eighteenth century, the writer expresses his astonishment at the fate of a people who, unlike the Muslims, did not have a divine revealed law, and were therefore reduced to the pitiable expedient of enacting their own laws.[9]

Laws based on 'borrowed morality' tend to lead to tyranny because their adherents cannot understand, and therefore cannot stomach, dissent – especially, I think, reasoned dissent, which is more likely to be challenging.[10] But rules and orders based on such a morality, fathered by the command theory, are liable anyway to be challenged, because the subject's power of reason and instinct for freedom will often struggle to push them aside. The command theory is thus a recipe for division. The ruler's responses may be tempered by the claims of mercy, but that is largely a matter of luck. In any case, no amount of mercy can of itself dislodge such ideologies from the thrones where their acolytes have crowned them. But law should never go unquestioned; it should therefore be a first principle for any State committed to the promotion of just government in a free polity that it must not base its legal arrangements on ideologies. This truth is celebrated and upheld, for example, in Article 2(1) of the Czech Charter of Fundamental Rights and Freedoms: 'The State is founded on democratic values and must not be bound either by an exclusive ideology or by a particular religion' (but democracy – and therefore 'democratic values' – needs careful handling: see chapter 2).

It is in any case an inherent feature of unruly humankind that what benefits the people will always be contentious. The suggestion that the public good inheres in a unique set of ideas that can be conclusively ascertained is contradicted by reason

---

[8] W James, *The Varieties of Religious Experience* (Longmans, Green & Co, 1902) Lecture XIII, 312. (The book reproduces James's Gifford Lectures, delivered at Edinburgh in 1901–02.)

[9] B Lewis, *What Went Wrong? Western Impact and Middle Eastern Response* (Phoenix, 2002) 127.

[10] The fawning corruption – repugnant to any dissent – that infects the close acolytes of a tyrannous dictator is well illustrated by the television series *Hitler's Circle of Evil* (2018).

and experience. The notion of a single exclusive truth takes wing only as an article of faith, secular or religious. It cannot be translated into a recipe for government save at the price of tyranny and therefore brutality. Treated as an article of faith it offers, moreover, a spurious justification for suppression and arbitrary rule: hence the wisdom of Havel's saying.

The error of a blind ideology is illuminated by a famous dilemma. It is to be found in Plato's dialogue, the *Euthyphro*. This is one of the dialogues that deal with Socrates' trial, condemnation and death in 399 BC at the hands of the restored Athenian democracy. Socrates says to his young friend Euthyphro, for whom the dialogue is named:

> Just consider this question: is that which is holy loved by the gods because it is holy, or is it holy because it is loved by the gods?[11]

Euthyphro's dilemma has been recycled many times in debates about religious, moral and political authority. In the religious context it may be rephrased thus:

> Are moral acts willed by God because they are good, or are they good because they are willed by God?

In the political context, we may restate the dilemma in this way:

> Are laws or policies willed by the State because they are good, or are they good because they are willed by the State?

The dilemma points up a striking contrast between two opposing views of value. The first is that the ascertainment of what is good is a function of man's reason and other characteristics of humankind, of which I shall have more to say. The second is that goodness is an axiom, a given, dictated by an external force: a blind ideology.

The ideologues are on the wrong side of Euthyphro's dilemma. We have to give the lie to the absolute authority of the book, whether it is scripture or politics. In some ways that is not an entirely comfortable conclusion. It will be seen as a challenge to religious faith, or at any rate to some of faith's varieties. Many good people – Christian, Muslim, Jewish and others – (as well as many less good) take a strict or literal view of scriptural authority. The difficulties are mitigated in the Anglican tradition by its threefold appeal to scripture, tradition and reason, which Richard Hooker, appointed Master of the Temple in 1585 and perhaps the greatest of English theologians, brought to its flourishing in his great work, *Of the Laws of Ecclesiastical Polity*.[12] I think some other religious traditions have been much less fortunate. A holy book must surely be a source of example and inspiration. If it is treated as anything like a rule book, full of commands that are not to be

---

[11] Plato, *Euthyphro*, 10A, tr HN Fowler (Loeb Classical Library, 1921).
[12] R Hooker, *Of the Laws of Ecclesiastical Polity*, ed AS McGrade (Oxford University Press, 2013).

questioned, it does not elevate humankind but enslaves it, or at least those who swallow its precepts without thinking for themselves.

The command theory nurtures the modern phenomenon of extremism: or rather extremism's modern forms, for there has always been what we now call extremism. It is a dangerous enemy of a just polity which aims to secure human rights and fundamental freedoms for its citizens, and it needs to be recognised as such.

Fundamentalist religious belief – that is, religious faith based on an unquestioning adherence to an imperative text held to be sacred (perhaps held to be the literal word of God) – is especially prone to the command theory. So are autocratic or dictatorial political regimes, in which for one reason or another the word of the ruler has acquired the mantle of sacred text.[13] I shall have more to say about religion in chapter 9.

But ideology is not always the child of the command theory. Not all ideologues are in its grip. Some, certainly, are brought up already trapped, with no real chance of escape. Some feel the pull of a master but do not give in all at once, at the price, perhaps, of real struggle with themselves. Some fall into the chasm through fear, or hate or hopelessness. Some have thought about it and seemed to decide – influenced, no doubt, by others – that it speaks truth or wisdom. Sometimes they can be persuaded otherwise. At least there is more hope of doing so than with ideologues who are entirely in the grip of the command theory.

As there are degrees of ideologues, so there are degrees of ideology itself. It does not always consist solely – as I put it earlier – in a preconception or preconceptions, an assumption or assumptions, not tested by reason, by argument, by practice or by results; an *a priori* belief, given or imposed in advance, assumed to be true. There may be a penumbra of reality, twisted into a belief, a doctrine, that is extreme or unreasonable. A State whose constitution is not controlled by the constitutional balance is more vulnerable to the growth of this kind of diluted ideology, and ultimately to the full-blown version.

II. Three Aspects of the Human Condition

Repudiation of the command theory and of blind ideology is the first step towards an ascertainment of the constitutional balance, and therefore the good constitution. But there is an associated point of some importance. To reject the command theory – to be on the right side of Euthyphro's dilemma – indeed to reject blind

---

[13] Such regimes, moreover, are almost always hypocritical, deploying doublespeak to support the gun, the bomb, and the grenade: 'euphemism also helped resolve the ultimate paradox which lay at the heart of Nazi ideology, between the regime's self-image as a guarantor of legality, and its desire to wipe out any opposition through untrammelled violence' (M Mazower, *Inside Hitler's Greece* (Yale University Press, 1993) 191).

ideology whether or not foisted by the command theory, by no means implies that the State's governance, or for that matter the structure of personal morals, is to be cast adrift on a sea of subjective opinion where anything goes if you happen to believe in it. In place of ideology we need to hone and develop, not mere preferences, but ideals – ideals that, unlike ideologies, are tested by argument, by practice, by results. Such ideals will of necessity reflect aspects of the human condition. The search for such ideals has, of course, occupied centuries of literature and learning. I shall only suggest – because it leads to what I shall say about the constitutional balance – that in this context three aspects of the human condition[14] seem to me to be of prime importance: (i) man is a rational being, (ii) he possesses free will, and (iii) he lives in society, in communion with others of his own kind.

As for the first of these, there are of course many people who through misfortune or vice are by no means rational; but the rational man is the paradigm. As for the second, the postulate of free will entails the rejection of philosophical determinism. For present purposes I shall have to take that for granted. I shall say only that determinism rules out choice and therefore responsibility – except as delusions. Thus it also negates any real, as opposed to imagined, conception of good and bad. Man is merely a machine. The falsity of determinism is a necessary condition of our very conception of ourselves as persons. It is the premise of every aspect of our social intercourse that depends on the use of reason. It is therefore also a necessary condition for the existence of a system of law and government. The third aspect – man's community with others of his kind – creates the obvious necessity of interaction with each other with all the emotions that entails; and we bring reason and free will to the process. There are of course solitary individuals, but society, again, is the paradigm.

These three horizons of the human condition require us to come to terms with each other. At every turn the individual is faced with choices that affect his fellows, who will judge him and make their own choices. Such judgements and choices define the culture in which their makers live; and it is only when they rest on such ideals as self-restraint, honesty, mutual respect and fair treatment that the culture in question has any hope of being at peace with itself. Without such anchors man cannot live in a free society, save at the price of endless insecurity; each person will fear his stronger neighbour; the currency of all their dealings will be brutality and distrust. These anchors, these ideals, are the very condition upon which human society is tolerable. They are the touchstones, at least they are among the touchstones, upon which other principles are honed and sharpened. They are critical to the values that govern civic or political society. They are the beginnings of a guide to how we ought to live.

---

[14] Cf HLA Hart, *The Concept of Law*, 3rd edn, eds J Raz and PA Bulloch (Oxford University Press, 2012).

I realise of course that everything I have so far said is merely at the surface of much deeper discussions. These reflections are intended as no more than signposts towards the subject of this book – the constitutional balance as the medium through which democracy and the Rule of Law, largely by means of the judicial review jurisdiction, become a unified force in the service of just government in a free polity.

III. Three Constitutional Fundamentals: The Constitutional Balance

The three horizons of the power of reason, free will and community point towards the construction of principles that will yield the constitutional balance. I take it as self-evident that the government of the State is to be conducted in the interests of the people, not the ruler. In that case the State's constitutional fundamentals, and therefore the balance between the Rule of Law and democracy, must reflect the people's own characteristics. Now, the relation between the laws of the State and the needs and aspirations of the people is of course the stuff of politics, and endlessly controversial. It is all the more important to identify the ground rules of the constitution under which the controversies of politics are to be conducted. They will be at a high level of generality, as will any viable description of the characteristics of the people which the constitution must reflect. Those characteristics, I think, are sufficiently represented for present purposes by the three factors to which I have referred: the power of reason, free will and community.

These three factors may then lead us to articulate the constitutional fundamentals of a civilized State, the principles that fuel the rule of law on the one hand and the rule of the popular vote on the other, and the balance between the two. The crossover between the human condition and constitutional principle has to be close, since otherwise there is a corrosive mismatch between the proper or natural aspirations of the people and the rules by which they are governed. I would identify the resulting constitutional fundamentals that the crossover gives us as reason (here, I mean reason in the making and application of the law and more generally the exercise of public power), fairness and the presumption of liberty.[15] These are the three horizons of the law of the constitution. They provide the higher premise, or at least part of it, that mandates obedience to the law. They are imposed by the Rule of Law (to which I shall turn in chapter 1) upon action by the State. Their moral force, translated into legal power, constrains democracy's exuberance. They are critical to the constitutional balance. I shall discuss them in detail in chapter 5.

---

[15] I have written before of these fundamentals: see J Laws, 'The Constitution: Morals and Rights' [1996] *PL* 622.

These three fundamentals are at the heart of our public law, and therefore of the judicial review jurisdiction. They are involved in a continual struggle between different interests, all of which are the proper concerns of the State. Often they are contradicted by political aspirations; policies that seem good to a popular government may wound the electorate or part of it and rub salt in the wound. Sometimes – as in times of national crisis or emergency – the claims of these three pillars may have to be cut down to size, so that executive decisions are allowed an increased latitude: but that is the constitutional balance at work. And it is no doubt obvious that what is reasonable, what is fair, what justifies State interference with individual liberty will strike different people very differently. All that said, the three pillars reach a long way. They imply the imposition of limits upon the actions of the State, and therefore upon the reach of democratic government. In the United Kingdom this discipline takes concrete form through the value-laden process of statutory interpretation by the judges – especially through the process of judicial review – by which the three pillars are supported in the face of inter-pretations that would undermine them; through the contrast between the Kantian morality of justice and the utilitarian morality of government, to which I shall come in chapter 3; and through the ups-and-downs of debate over the traditional doctrine of the sovereignty of Parliament (chapter 8).

The constitutional balance describes the whole of this arena. In this jurisdic-tion it consists in the reconciliations furnished by the common law to all these confrontations. It measures and balances the interests of the citizen and the State where they are in conflict, and the contrasting powers of the courts and the elected government.

Although my focus is on the English common law, and in particular on the judicial review jurisdiction, the dilemmas the constitutional balance confronts are surely universal. They do not merely vex those States that lay claim to liberal democracy. No less inevitably they pressurise autocracies, even though all too often they are despised, ignored or contradicted. It would be wrong to suppose that the constitutional balance merely represents an antithesis between democracy and dictatorship. It is much more likely to be achieved in a democracy, but totalitarian government is not always or necessarily tyrannous – rule for the ruler's sake. An autocrat may truly believe that his actions serve his people. Sometimes, with great good fortune, the autocrat may even be right. I said earlier that it is a matter of chance, of luck, whether the master's command is bad or good. Consider Gibbon's view of the Emperors of Rome in the first and second centuries AD:

> If a man were called to fix the period in the history of the world, during which the condition of the human race was most happy and prosperous, he would, without hesitation, name that which elapsed from the death of Domitian to the accession of Commodus. The vast extent of the Roman empire was governed by absolute power, under the guidance of virtue and wisdom. The armies were restrained by the firm but gentle hand of four successive emperors, whose characters and authority commanded involuntary respect. The forms of the civil administration were carefully preserved by Nerva, Trajan, Hadrian, and the Antonines, who delighted in the image of liberty, and

were pleased with considering themselves as the accountable ministers of the laws. Such princes deserved the honour of restoring the republic, had the Romans of their days been capable of enjoying a rational freedom.[16]

Dreamland perhaps. Such a benign autocracy, in the very unlikely event of its happening, is an uncovenanted blessing. It is no doubt significant that the emperors thus praised by Gibbon clothed their rule with the trappings of republican legality – 'pleased with considering themselves as the accountable ministers of the laws'; though the sting in the tail is no less telling – 'had the Romans of their days been capable of enjoying a rational freedom'.

IV. The Scheme of the Book

Now I shall summarise the scheme of the chapters that follow. I have already referred to some. Some (not least chapter 5) are largely concerned with the substance of the law, and contain a good deal of case law.

In chapter 1, I shall give an account of the Rule of Law. This is the first step towards an ascertainment of the constitutional balance. The subject has generated a vast literature, but there is a remarkable lack of consensus as to what it means, though it has great resonance: certainly as a totem, even a rallying cry. I shall explain what I mean by it from a common law perspective and, in doing so, foreshadow the constitutional fundamentals of reason, fairness and the presumption of liberty that, as I have said, I shall discuss more fully in chapter 5.

In chapter 2, I turn to democracy: the other side of the balance. I shall say that, like the Roman god Janus, it has two faces: its virtue is as a prophylactic against tyranny, but its vice is its openness to short-term, populist measures. It owes both faces to the sanction of the ballot-box. It is certainly no guarantor of good or wise substantive law.

In chapter 3 I shall confront the contrasting moralities of law and politics, or courts and government: as I have said, the morality of law is Kantian, that of politics utilitarian. The former is centred on the autonomy of every individual, the latter on the interests or well-being of the people as a whole. Both are necessary in the good constitution. The benign tension between them conditions and restrains both the force of constitutional principle and the force of governmental power. They are therefore critical to the constitutional balance.

In chapter 4, I describe the common law's place in our constitution, and what I shall describe as its fourfold methodology. This is important for the role of judicial review, and more generally to demonstrate the historic utility of the common law as an engine of the constitutional balance.

---

[16] E Gibbon, *Decline and Fall of the Roman Empire*, vol I (Penguin Random House, 2010) ch III, pt 2.

In chapter 5, as I have indicated, I shall give an account of the constitutional fundamentals of reason, fairness and the presumption of liberty: government decision-making without them, or any of them, would be barbarous. These are the principles that promote the claims of law to constrain the elected power. The presumption of liberty, as I shall show, is a more complex idea than at first appears.

Chapter 6 takes a concrete aspect of the constitutional balance further: I shall consider the extent to which the courts should on a principled basis defer to the policy claims of government, and shall turn to some of the case law to see how in practice the courts have described the notion of judicial deference, and thus sought to find the limit or the edge of public power; this is critical to the constitutional balance.

Chapter 7 addresses what I regard as two fundamental mistakes in the theory and practice of our constitutional law. The first is the concept of parliamentary intention. The second is what has come to be called the *ultra vires* theory of judicial review: the notion 'that judicial review is legitimated on the ground that the courts are applying the intent of the legislature'.[17] As I shall show, the refutation of both is of the first importance for the recognition and establishment of the constitutional balance. Both of these ideas undermine the vital pillars of the constitution – reason, fairness and the presumption of liberty – because they deliver them to the whim of the legislators for the time being.

In chapter 8 I shall turn to the dilemmas of the English doctrine of the sovereignty of Parliament. The doctrine creates an obvious conundrum for the constitutional balance: how is the democratic power to be kept true to the balance if the legislature is all-powerful? The two mistakes that I seek to correct in chapter 7 are important for a proper understanding of legislative sovereignty.

Chapter 9 is on human rights, free thought and speech. I shall give some account of how the law of human rights plays its part in the constitutional balance, and the ways in which it may threaten the balance. Free thought and speech are a vital antithesis to blind ideology. Free thought – which needs free expression to survive – is a condition of every person's flourishing, and is demanded by our constitutional fundamentals.

In the conclusions at the end of each chapter, I shall try to bring all these interlocking themes together.

V. Reflections

There are of course many functions of the law and dimensions of the State which this book is not about. But the balance between individual rights and freedoms on

---

[17] P Craig, 'Ultra Vires and the Foundations of Judicial Review' (1998) 57(1) *CLJ* 63, 64.

the one hand and the general public interest on the other – which is at the centre of the constitutional balance – is by no means the exclusive territory of judicial review. In particular it gives shape and content to the law of crime. And it requires the law to determine another balance in which the State has a lively concern: that between the rights and interests of one citizen and those of another. To that extent the constitutional balance also informs the whole *corpus* of private law. The practical effects of the law of crime and the law of civil disputes will no doubt affect the attitudes of thinking citizens and government to the question where the constitutional balance should be drawn.

Though these themes bear on the constitutional balance, they are outside the range of this book. I acknowledge other limitations: I said earlier that my opening comments on the vice of ideology, and what I have called three aspects of the human condition, are merely at the surface of much deeper discussions. There is of course much literature on the subject of scriptural authority, philosophical determinism and the freedom of the will, moral responsibility and the proper role of the State. I can only hope that the idea of the constitutional balance may provide something of a weathervane in face of the conflicting forces that batter the constitution of a free polity, and that it may be seen as an important determinant of civilised rule.

I do not claim to discover or articulate the *best* constitution. That postulates a political Elysian field, where every question is finally resolved and further enquiry has no purpose. In the sphere of moral and political values, the notion that there is nothing left to argue about is as arrogant as it is depressing, a bilious mixture. Such a vision recalls John Donne's dreadful picture of heaven – 'where there shall be no darkness nor dazzling, but one equal light; no noise nor silence, but one equal music; no fears nor hopes, but one equal possession; no ends nor beginnings, but one equal eternity':[18] a place where nothing ever changes – hell, not heaven. We should celebrate the fact that there is so much more to discover; that we are not the masters of the universe. The good constitution can be no more than the best we can presently envisage, given what we presently know of the human condition.

---

[18] John Donne (1571–1631), Dean of St Paul's Cathedral, Prayer, 'Our Last Awakening', available at https://www.stmw.org/donne.html.

1

The Rule of Law

In order to understand how the constitutional balance is to work, we need to be clear what we mean by the Rule of Law. It has provoked a vast and contrary literature. One reason is that like the Hydra, it has many heads. Some are uncontentious. No civilised person doubts the need for fair systems of civil and criminal justice, fairly but firmly enforced. But the debates about the Rule of Law have generally been conducted at what might be called a more strategic level. Here too there is agreement to begin with: State power must be exercised in accordance with promulgated, non-retrospective law made according to established procedures. There is a nice story told by Blackstone. Peter the Great's Ambassador was arrested and taken out of his coach in London for an unpaid debt. Though some of those who had arrested him were imprisoned, the Czar

> resented this affront very highly, and demanded that the sheriff of Middlesex and all others concerned in the arrest should be punished with instant death. But the queen (to the amazement of that despotic court) directed her secretary to inform him 'that she could inflict no punishment upon any, the meanest, of her subjects, unless warranted by the law of the land …'[1]

So far so good, but the question that has enlivened argument amongst academics and others is whether the Rule of Law involves, or should involve, *more* than an insistence on promulgated law.

Before going any further there is a preliminary point to be made about the nature of this enquiry into the Rule of Law. The question, 'What is the Rule of Law?' looks like a search for some factual reality – if only we ponder long and hard enough, sift the evidence, study all the material, at length we may find out what it actually is. But that is not at all the nature of the exercise. The Rule of Law is not a fact, or an event or a thing. It is the name of a value, or an ideal: highly practical, but a value or an ideal nonetheless. We have to decide what is the nature of this ideal to which we choose to give the name, the Rule of Law. It is not a voyage of discovery. We are not following map; we are drawing it. We are not investigating what is, but what ought to be. It is not a matter of dictionary definitions. The lexicographers do not have the key to the Rule of Law. We cannot find it out by looking it up. We have to *choose* what we shall call the Rule of Law. It is not given

---

[1] W Blackstone, *Commentaries on the Laws of England*, Book I (Clarendon Press, 1765) 255.

to us. The need to find it out, to *create* it, exemplifies the imperative I described in the Introduction: the denial of ideologies, and of the command theory of moral conduct: the duty to hone and develop tested ideals.

The Rule of Law was once not very much more than an expression used by academics, prominent in Professor AV Dicey's seminal but much criticised work, *The Law of the Constitution*, first published in 1885.[2] Indeed it may be said that Dicey practically invented the expression. Sir Stephen Sedley[3] has found only one instance of its use before Dicey, in a case in 1636, when Mr Justice Berkeley said this:

> There is a Rule of Law and a rule of government, and things that may not be done by the Rule of Law may be done by the rule of government.

I am not sure what Berkeley J meant; to the modern ear it sounds very sinister.

As a concept of government, for a long time the Rule of Law held no surpassing interest for political rulers. It gained little attention even among the judges. In recent years, however, in the United Kingdom (UK) and elsewhere, it has taken its place as a fundamental constitutional principle. Section 1 of the UK statute, the Constitutional Reform Act 2005, proclaims 'This Act does not adversely affect – (a) the existing constitutional principle of the rule of law'. On the dust jacket of Lord Bingham's book, *The Rule of Law*,[4] there are printed four quotations in which the words 'the Rule of Law' appear: one from Barack Obama, one from David Cameron, one from Tony Blair and one from Margaret Thatcher. The Rule of Law has acquired great resonance. It has become a slogan.

I. Two Meanings of the Rule of Law

The meaning of the Rule of Law is, however, strikingly elusive; there is no consensus, at least no overall consensus, on the subject. Despite its grand protestation in section 1, the Constitutional Reform Act 2005 does not tell us what the Rule of Law is (or what our legislators think it is). For some it is a Protean conception. That approach is exemplified by Lord Bingham's Sir David Williams[5] lecture *The Rule of Law*, delivered on 16 November 2006, from which, as Lord Bingham said in the Preface, he drew heavily in coming to write his book on the subject, published in 2010.

---

[2] JWF Allison (ed), *AV Dicey, The Law of the Constitution* (Oxford: Oxford University Press, 2013), pp 1–213.

[3] S Sedley, *Lions Under the Throne* (Cambridge University Press, 2015) ch 14, 274–75.

[4] T Bingham, *The Rule of Law* (Allen Lane, 2010).

[5] Professor Sir David Williams QC died on 6 September 2009. He is mourned by lawyers and by many others, not only for his conspicuous intellectual gifts, but also for his warmth and his humour, which lightened many assemblies. He graced the conference on judicial review held in Hong Kong in December 2008, jointly organised by the Public Law Centre at Cambridge and the law faculty of the Chinese University of Hong Kong.

There is as I have said an agreed beginning: the uncontentious proposition, which I stated at the outset, that State power must be exercised in accordance with promulgated, non-retrospective law made according to established procedures. Some regard this as all that the Rule of Law requires (in addition, presumably, to effective enforcement procedures). This has often been called the 'thin' theory of the Rule of Law. But as an overarching constitutional principle, if it stands alone this is very weak soup indeed; for although it insists on the virtues of legal certainty and accessibility, and of compliance with the law, it insists on nothing else. In his book Lord Bingham cites[6] Professor Raz's description of the thin theory operating in extreme circumstances as follows:

> A non-democratic legal system, based on the denial of human rights, on extensive poverty, on racial segregation, sexual inequalities, and religious persecution may, in principle, conform to the requirements of the Rule of Law better than any of the legal systems of the more enlightened Western democracies ... It will be an immeasurably worse legal system, but it will excel in one respect: in its conformity to the Rule of Law ... The law may ... institute slavery without violating the Rule of Law.[7]

There is another sense frequently attributed to the Rule of Law. This is what has been called the 'thick' theory. The 'thick' theorists hold that the Rule of Law is not satisfied unless the content of the laws is virtuous. In these days they will usually include the values of fair procedure, proportionality and a panoply of human rights. This would seem to be Lord Bingham's position. In his book he expresses it thus:

> While, therefore, one can recognize the logical force of Professor Raz's contention, I would roundly reject it in favour of a 'thick' definition, embracing the protection of human rights within its scope. A state which savagely represses or persecutes sections of its people cannot in my view be regarded as observing the Rule of Law, even if the transport of the persecuted minority to the concentration camp or the compulsory exposure of female children on the mountainside is the subject of detailed laws duly enacted and scrupulously observed.[8]

The thin theory and the thick theory are both defective. The first proves too little and the second proves too much. The thin theory offers a standard of legality that, given Professor Raz's nightmare scenario, is hardly worth having if it is taken on its own: it is, to say the least, morally unambitious. But the thick theory collapses the Rule of Law into whatever set of socio-political norms, capable of being enforced by law, is favoured by any theorist who thinks about the matter; and in that case the Rule of Law lacks any distinctive meaning and is not an autonomous principle. Lord Bingham explains what his 'thick' view amounts to in practice under eight heads. They include social goods, such as good faith on the part of public powers, and the protection of human rights.

---

[6] Bingham (n 4) ch7, 66.
[7] J Raz, 'The Rule of Law and its Virtue' in J Raz, *The Authority of Law: Essays on Law and Morality* (Oxford University Press, 1979) 211, 221.
[8] Bingham (n 4) 67.

They are, in truth, a suggested list of the virtues of a decent nation State. You may very likely agree with the list; but it fails to capture the distinct quality or characteristic which the *law* – the Rule of Law – provides or contributes. Lord Bingham's assertion that '[a] state which savagely represses or persecutes sections of its people cannot in my view be regarded as observing the Rule of Law' is just that: an assertion.

II. The Rule of Law – Where Next?

How then is the Rule of Law to be properly understood? First, if it is to be of any value, it must *include* the thin theory. Promulgated, non-retrospective law made according to established procedures is a bare minimum requirement for any State in which the people are to be saved from capricious and despotic rule. But that is only a necessary, not a sufficient condition for the avoidance of tyranny. The quotation from Raz appears to show that a State may observe a meticulous obedience to the thin theory and still promulgate and enforce a collection of social philosophies every one of which is deeply nasty. I say *appears* to show: I shall argue shortly that the thin theory is not so self-contained.

However that may be, the thin theory of the Rule of Law seems to contribute little to the constitutional balance. It restrains political power (to the extent that it does so at all) only by its insistence on proper procedures for the making and application of the law. Most of us would want to understand law as possessing some more substantial virtue. Cicero thought that the morality of law was inherent or original: 'It is clear that laws were originally made for the security of the people, for the preservation of cities, for the peace and benefit of society'.[9] But how are we to enlarge law's virtue without causing it to collapse into whatever catalogue of social goods happens to meet with our approval – the mistake of the thick theory?

III. Independent and Impartial Adjudication

The first point here is to recognise that the thin theory itself implies or requires more than it seems to state. As I have foreshadowed, it is not self-contained. It requires that the judges must ensure, and have the power to ensure, that State action falls within the terms of the relevant published law. This appears to be no more than a modest contribution to the constitutional balance. But that is not the whole of it. Judicial supervision of State action, however modest, must

---

[9] Cicero, *De Legibus*, 2.11.

be meaningful. It must therefore be in the hands of independent and impartial judges. Unless the judges are independent and impartial, there is no point in having them; since if they are not, their decisions have no more value than if they were made by the reviewed body itself.

In passing I shall just say this about independence and impartiality. Much has been written about it. By independence I mean simply that the judge is not in the grip or pocket of anyone. By impartiality I mean that he or she comes to every case with as open a mind as humanity allows, and with no axe of his or her own or of his or her friends to grind. There is a wonderful story, repeated by Sir Stephen Sedley in his collection of essays,[10] about a judge called Sir Thomas Jones, who was Chief Justice of the Common Pleas in the time of James II. In 1686 the King sought to pack the court that was to decide the case[11] about the legality of his use of the dispensing power to allow Roman Catholics to hold military commissions. He told Sir Thomas Jones that he must give up either his opinion or his place. Here is Sir Thomas's reply:

> For my place I care little. I am old and worn out in the service of the Crown. But I am mortified to find that Your Majesty thinks me capable of giving a judgment which none but an ignorant or a dishonest man could give ... Your Majesty may find twelve judges of your mind, but hardly twelve lawyers.[12]

Perhaps it is obvious that even in the scenario of the thin theory, there must be independent and impartial judges. But the point goes further than at first appears. The State's acceptance of an independent and impartial judiciary implies a deeper acceptance: an acceptance that the judges will apply objective standards to the task of adjudication, *and that these standards will condition the meaning of the laws that are the subject of adjudication.* This is true even in the minimalist vision of the thin theory. The meaning of any given law may be – very often will be – uncertain. Not always: sometimes there are straightforward cases where the meaning is unambiguous. A tax rate may be set at x pence in the pound and that will be that (though what circumstances generate the liability to pay may of course be highly contentious). But very many statutes, perhaps most, lack this luxury of specificity. They deal with issues having many layers, all of whose implications cannot be foreseen and may even be contradictory. In such cases, one interpretation may be more repugnant even to the modest principles of the thin theory (to say nothing of anything more ambitious) than another. The statute's meaning must be independently decided; and the judge making the decision, though of course he or she will start with the text, will as likely as not be bound to proceed to a value judgment as to the law's complicity with basic norms which the text does not, and cannot, provide. If the text does not give the whole answer, there is no other recourse.

---

[10] Sedley (n 3) 131.

[11] *Godden v Hales* (1686) 11 St Tr 1165.

[12] CH Firth (ed), *Macaulay, The History of England from the Accession of James II* (1914 ed), vol II, p 735, discussed and in part quoted by AW Bradley, 'Relations between executive, judiciary and Parliament: an evolving saga?' [2008] *PL* 470 at pp 481–82.

Professor Trevor Allan, in *The Sovereignty of Law*,[13] I think goes some way to an acknowledgement of this position:

> On that view [ie the thin theory], the judicial role is simply to enforce whatever rules have been duly enacted by the legislature, without fear or favour: all are subject to the law, whatever its content, according to its enacted terms and without special exemptions (not expressly enacted) for powerful officials or their friends and allies.[14]

Enforcement of the law without fear or favour, or special exemptions for friends or allies, brings to the process of interpretation a value – an objective standard – that lies beyond the unqualified interests of the lawmaker. It therefore transcends the thin theory pure and simple; or at least it demonstrates that the thin theory is more than it seems.

This approach is also, I think, implicitly supported by Dicey. In chapter XIII of *The Law of the Constitution* we find this:

> The fact that the most arbitrary powers of the English executive must always be exercised under Act of Parliament places the government, even when armed with the widest authority, under the supervision, so to speak, of the Courts. Powers, however extraordinary, which are conferred or sanctioned by statute, are never really unlimited, for they are confined by the words of the Act itself, and, what is more, by the interpretation put upon the statute by the judges. Parliament is supreme legislator, but from the moment Parliament has uttered its will as lawgiver, that will becomes subject to the interpretation put on it by the judges of the land, and the judges, who are influenced by the feelings of magistrates no less than by the general spirit of the common law, are disposed to construe statutory exceptions to common law principles in a mode which would not commend itself either to a body of officials, or to the Houses of Parliament, if the Houses were called upon to interpret their own enactments. In foreign countries, and especially in France, administrative ideas – notions derived from the traditions of a despotic monarchy – have restricted the authority and to a certain extent influenced the ideas of the judges. In England judicial notions have modified the action and influenced the ideas of the executive government. By every path we come round to the same conclusion, that Parliamentary sovereignty has favoured the Rule of Law, and that the supremacy of the law of the land both calls forth the exertion of Parliamentary sovereignty, and leads to its being exercised in spirit of legality.[15]

One may perhaps contrast the saying ascribed to Frederick the Great: 'My people and I have come to an agreement which satisfies us both. They are to say what they please, and I am to do what I please.'

---

[13] TRS Allen, *The Sovereignty of Law* (Oxford University Press, 2013) 2.
[14] ibid.
[15] Dicey (n 2) 183–84. Professor David Feldman drew my attention to this passage.

IV. Beyond the Thin Theory

Perhaps it is obvious enough that even the thin theory needs more than independent and impartial courts. It requires also that the content and application of the law be imbued with certain norms, standards or principles. This very requirement, however, demolishes the thin theory as a free-standing account of the Rule of Law. Independent judges who are committed to the vindication of promulgated, non-retrospective law made according to established procedures are of necessity committed also to principles that justify that vindication. Otherwise their commitment is meaningless. But such principles cannot be limited to the service of the thin theory's limited values. They are grounded in a wider ideal. In general terms the ideal may be described as the protection of the individual citizen's autonomy. He or she is not to be thrown from pillar to post by State authority without reason, without knowing why and without the right to answer back. The citizen is to be protected from capricious power because he or she has a value of his or her own. He or she is not the State's creature. Even the thin theory acknowledges as much. But the principle goes wider. The citizen must be treated justly, and must have a voice.

The value, the autonomy, of the individual is of course old philosophy: Christian, Kantian and central to many other traditions besides. It is contradicted in dictatorships, religious or political. It is testimony to the vice of ideologies and to the falsity of the command theory of moral conduct to which, as I said in the Introduction, fundamentalist religious positions and dictatorial regimes are especially prone. My purpose is not to extol it by a journey over well-trodden ground. My point is that in the context of lawgiving it is a foundation of the constitutional balance, for it requires constraint of the power of government – including democratic government. At once, therefore, we are in the territory of the constitutional pillars of reason, fairness and the presumption of liberty. Their moral force, translated into legal power, constrains democracy's exuberance. They are at the core of the constitutional balance. But it is critical to understand that these pillars are not erected, and the unruly idea of the individual citizen's autonomy is not given or guaranteed, by the political ideal of democracy itself. I shall turn to democracy in chapter 2.

V. *Unison v Lord Chancellor*

There is, if I may say so, a very learned disquisition on the Rule of Law in Lord Reed's judgment in *Unison v Lord Chancellor*.[16] The issue was whether fees imposed by the Lord Chancellor by the Employment Tribunals and the

---

[16] *Unison v Lord Chancellor* [2017] UKSC 51 [67] et seq.

Employment Appeal Tribunal Fees Order 2013,[17] in respect of proceedings in employment tribunals and the employment appeal tribunal, were unlawful because of their effects on access to justice. Lord Reed cites a good deal of authority on access to justice,[18] and more generally on the Rule of Law. For my purpose the judgment is particularly helpful for its account of the importance of access to justice. It shows, albeit indirectly, that access to the Queen's courts is a precondition of the constitutional balance. I shall give just one citation:

> Courts exist in order to ensure that the laws made by Parliament, and the common law created by the courts themselves, are applied and enforced. That role includes ensuring that the executive branch of government carries out its functions in accordance with the law. In order for the courts to perform that role, people must in principle have unimpeded access to them. Without such access, laws are liable to become a dead letter, the work done by Parliament may be rendered nugatory, and the democratic election of Members of Parliament may become a meaningless charade. That is why the courts do not merely provide a public service like any other.[19]

This account omits any reference to the courts' role as constitutional lawgivers, but Lord Reed's observations on the effect on democratic government if access to justice were denied demonstrate that in such circumstances the constitutional balance would simply be impossible: 'the work done by Parliament may be rendered nugatory'.

As regards the substance of the case, Lord Reed held:

> In order for the fees to be lawful, they have to be set at a level that everyone can afford, taking into account the availability of full or partial remission. The evidence now before the court, considered realistically and as a whole, leads to the conclusion that that requirement is not met.[20]

The evidence before the court was detailed and complex, and much of the judgment is given to its examination. In the end, however, it seems to me that Lord Reed's conclusion that the Fees Order was unlawful was based on the surely conventional principle that access to justice is not to be denied without very specific statutory authority (and even then, at least in an extreme case, there might be a question whether the judicial oath might require the judges to depart from the statute (see chapter 8)).

The *Unison* case is also interesting because of the extended criticism directed at Lord Reed's judgment by Sir Stephen Laws, former First Parliamentary Counsel, in a paper entitled 'Second Guessing Policy Choices: The rule of law after the

---

[17] SI 2013/1893.
[18] See, eg, the references to Coke and Blackstone in *Unison* (n 16) [75]; but there is much more besides.
[19] ibid [68].
[20] ibid [91].

Supreme Court's UNISON judgment'.[21] The essence of his assault on Lord Reed's substantive conclusion is summarised in the first paragraph:

> [Lord Reed's judgment] represents a significant expansion of the concept of the rule of law: from a set of principles about how policy should be implemented, into a doctrine that operates, in practical terms, for regulating the content of public policy. The incontrovertible and sound principle that the executive must comply with the law transforms itself, in the reasoning of the judgment, into the idea that there are at least some areas of policy (the financial management of the justice system, it seems, is one) that are to be subjected to a judicial 'success test' under which the judiciary is able, with the benefit of hindsight, to second-guess and overturn political policy decisions by reference not to how they were made or implemented, but rather by reference to what, it turns out, has been their effect in practice.[22]

The criticism (like the judgment itself) is intricate, painstaking and very fully developed. Short citations cannot do it justice, but I will give one more:

> 10. The illegality of the Fees Order, Lord Reed said, arose because, quite simply, 'it *has the effect of* preventing access to justice', or because it, in practice, created, 'a real risk that persons will effectively be prevented from having access to justice'. Whichever of these tests is the main basis for the judgment, it is absolutely clear that substantial reliance was being placed on retrospectively testing the legality of the Fees Order (as at the time it was made) by reference to what turned out to be its subsequent effect in practice. The outcome of the case, it is made clear, does not depend on the identification of any failure by the Lord Chancellor, at or before the time of the making of the Fees Order, to consider its likely or foreseeable effect.[23]

I shall leave full argument on the merits of the judgment and the criticism to others (it would require a very long chapter on its own). I shall only say that it seems to me at present that it is a perfectly legitimate use of the judicial review jurisdiction to quash a decision that *turns out* to breach a constitutional principle such as access to justice, even if that was neither foreseen nor foreseeable by the decision-maker.

There is another aspect of Sir Stephen's essay that repays attention. He takes Lord Reed to task for isolating the legislative function from surrounding functions, not least the contribution of the executive, which have an important impact:

> The executive's initiative in legislative matters ... is reinforced by the custom and practice of the two Houses and by the practical effect of the Standing Orders and conventions about the arrangement of business.[24]

---

[21] Sir Stephen Laws, 'Second Guessing Policy Choices: The rule of law after the Supreme Court's UNISON judgment' (Policy Exchange, 14 March 2018) available at https://policyexchange.org.uk/wp-content/uploads/2018/03/Second-guessing-policy-choices-2.pdf.

[22] ibid 1, footnote omitted.

[23] ibid 9, footnotes omitted.

[24] ibid 31.

It seems to me that these surrounding functions, so far as they refine the legislative product, can only promote the constitutional balance.

VI. Two Basics: Normative Statutory Interpretation and the Individual's Autonomy

I said earlier that the meaning of any given law will often be uncertain, and the uncertainty can only be resolved by normative interpretation. The court has to bring a *value or values* to bear on the task of construction. I shall have more to say about the common law's means of doing so in chapter 4. This uncertainty is important: it is benign and inevitable. It is benign because it invites a partnership with constitutional principle: imagine a State where every statute was absolutely unambiguous. It would be a State in which every department of life the legislator chose to regulate would be regulated to the uttermost detail. As for the inevitability of uncertainty in statute – at least the likelihood of it in many cases – an eighteenth-century instance provides a striking illustration. *Omychund v Barker*,[25] decided in 1744, concerned a question whether the testimony of a witness who refused to swear a Christian oath could be received in English proceedings. Witnesses appearing before Commissioners in India would only swear in the manner of their 'Gentoo' (Hindu) religion, which was to touch the foot of a Brahmin priest with their hand. William Murray (later Lord Mansfield, at this time Solicitor General, but representing a private party in the proceedings) submitted that in the absence of precedent, 'the only question is whether upon principles of reason, justice, and convenience, this witness ought to be admitted'.[26] Then he said this:

> All occasions do not arise at once; now a particular species of Indians appears; hereafter another species of Indians may arise; a statute very seldom can take in all cases, therefore the common law, that works itself pure by rules drawn from the fountain of justice, is for this reason superior to an act of parliament.[27]

Not every statute can be interpreted solely by reference to its language. The exercise of statutory interpretation is very frequently value-laden, normative rather than descriptive. Legislation typically addresses broad positions; it cannot usually prescribe with exactitude the limits of its own application in every case; so the

---

[25] *Omychund v Barker* (1744) 26 Eng Rep 14. I owe this reference to Poser's excellent biography: NS Poser, *Lord Mansfield: Justice in the Age of Reason* (McGill-Queen's University Press, 2013) 99.
[26] *Omychund v Barker* (n 25) 22.
[27] ibid 22.

courts have to decide how the legislation is to be applied. Lord Mansfield's insight in *Omychund*'s case was to recognise that this process is not merely interpretive but evaluative. It is a creative process. It makes law. And once it is accepted that the process is in the hands of independent and impartial judges, it possesses an integrity of its own: that is, the law thus made will give effect to standards that are not merely the creatures of the ruler who made the laws.

Given all this, the way between the thin theory and the thick theory of the Rule of Law consists, I think, in the mediation of government edicts – in our constitution the statutes passed by Parliament – through constitutional principles kept by independent courts. They are part of what the Rule of Law actually *means*, and therefore at the core of the constitutional balance.

VII. Possible Objections

I shall confront two possible objections to what I have said so far. First, you might suppose that in Joseph Raz's nightmare instance of the thin theory, the judges who interpret the laws might not espouse liberal norms of the kind I have described as constitutional pillars. They will be creatures of a culture that places no value on such things. But the thin theory clearly attributes value to independent adjudication. Implicitly it acknowledges that without it there is no Rule of Law; and this is a critical limitation on the power of the ruler. In practice it means that the judge will always look for the edge, the limit, of the power the statute gives to the ruler, and will do so with no bias in the ruler's favour. If it were otherwise, the judge would merely be the ruler's cypher, his or her amanuensis. He or she would be neither independent nor impartial. But in that case, not even the thin theory would be satisfied. There would be no Rule of Law.

The second possible objection is this. It may be thought that the requirement of objective standards or norms, accepted because the place in the constitution of an independent and impartial judiciary is accepted, simply points back to the thick theory: it invites whatever code of good government happens to appeal to whoever is thinking about it. But the difference is that these standards are not merely a selection of social goods but a necessary function of the legal process itself, precisely because a statute's often uncertain text cannot take effect without the mediation of constitutional norms. The Rule of Law requires all the formal constraints of the thin theory: the law must be promulgated, accessible and (subject perhaps to certain carefully controlled exceptions) not retrospective. It also requires effective mechanisms of enforcement. But the Rule of Law transcends the thin theory, because the thin theory taken on its own cannot account for the *implication* of independent and impartial adjudication, namely the importation of constitutional norms into the process of statutory interpretation. That is by no means a collapse into the thick theory. The normative element in the Rule of Law is, as I have said, a necessary function of the legal process itself.

VIII. Examples

I shall note some familiar instances of constitutional norms at work in the interpretive process. Consider these familiar cases:

(a) Criminal statutes must be interpreted strictly. (The same used to be true of taxing statutes, although that, perhaps, is less clear nowadays.)

(b) The courts lean against retrospective applications.

The second vindicates an aspect of the thin theory. The first goes wider. These are both normative, not merely descriptive, positions; but they are part of the warp and weave of statutory construction. They, and many other nostrums of statutory interpretation, are norms for the regulation of the conduct of persons and bodies subject to the law in question. They are the creatures, not of any rule laid down by Parliament, but of successive judges' perceptions of what may reasonably be called foundational principles of the constitution. They constitute the objective standards imported by the judges, or at least they are those standards' paradigms. They bring us back directly to the constitutional pillars of reason, fairness and the presumption of liberty. Their moral force, translated into legal power, constrains democracy's exuberance. As I have said, they are part of what the Rule of Law actually *means*, and are therefore at the core of the constitutional balance.

IX. Conclusions

My view of the Rule of Law, then, is that the very process of impartial and independent adjudication (which even the thin theory requires) implies the deployment of objective standards in the interpretation and development of the law. The standards start with loyalty to the law's language – statute law should be interpreted according to the ordinary meaning of its text. But this is only a starting-point. Lord Mansfield's argument in *Omychund* exemplifies the truth that very often the language will not cover every case. No less often, the language may be capable of more than one interpretation. In all these instances the judges will apply standards that constitute norms for the regulation of the conduct of persons and bodies subject to the law in question. The core standards are reason, fairness and the presumption of liberty, whose practical application requires the constitutional balance.

It may strike the reader as curious that in all this discussion of constitutional principle and the Rule of Law I have not so far mentioned *justice*. Justice is of course at the centre of every aspect of our legal system – criminal law, private civil law, family law, enforcement process: though, as I said in the Introduction, these are among the many functions of the law which this book is not about. Justice is inherent in all of them, and all of them involve the inclusion of constitutional principles in the territory of statutory interpretation. The same principles – obviously perhaps – infuse judge-made law, that is, the creations of the common law that are independent of statute, and I shall say more about that in chapter 5. The insistence of justice is found in the second of our three core constitutional norms, fairness, and in chapter 5 I shall also return to that.

Lastly, the ideas of the Rule of Law, the good constitution, the constitutional balance, pose what might be called a social conundrum. Immanuel Kant said:

> We must not expect a good constitution because those who make it are moral men. Rather it is because of a good constitution that we may expect a society composed of moral men.[28]

I am not so sure. I think much depends on the temper of the people. But I am no anthropologist.

---

[28] Quoted by L Fuller, *The Morality of Law* (Yale University Press, rev edn 1969) 152.

2

Democracy

At the present day, the western political consensus is largely uncritical of representative democracy as a virtuous form of government. It is thought that democracy tends to invest the voice of the people not only with the power to throw out governments, but also with an adventitious wisdom (exaggerated if the State resorts to a referendum) about what government ought to do. In order to appreciate the relation between judicial and political power, and therefore the constitutional balance, we need to understand the merits and demerits of democracy. In this chapter I discuss the moral strengths and weaknesses of democratic government, the source of political power in this jurisdiction. To advance the discussion, I shall first say a little about its apparent opposite, autocratic government.

Autocratic government of course proceeds on the basis that some citizens – perhaps only one (the ruler), or a group defined by race, religion, sex, class or political affiliation – should possess entrenched rights altogether denied to the others. Dr Johnson said, 'A country governed by a despot is an inverted cone.'[1] Autocracy has in different forms enjoyed sway throughout human history, and remains prevalent in many corners of the globe. A principal modern manifestation, communist rule, pretends that the people are the ruler, which on the whole is less honest and more insidious than an assertion of outright autocracy.

But in principle there is nothing self-contradictory about autocracy. It may be justified in the ruler's mind by the pleasure of ruling, and the extent to which he or she may bleed the people to satisfy himself or herself. Or it may seem to be justified by the ruler's belief – which others may share – that his or her rule is beneficent, and that any other form of government would be to the people's disadvantage. It is worth noting that this is not always a false belief. In the Introduction, I cited Gibbon's observations about the Roman Emperors between Domitian and Commodus. Some varieties of autocracy have in their time brought great benefits. Some autocrats have done great good. You can multiply the list of beneficent autocrats. You might include the Emperor Augustus, who transformed the Roman Republic into a principate; and Henry II of England, who first sent the judges round the English shires (although the record of both rulers is very far from untarnished). The name of King Solomon of Israel has passed into our language as a byword for wisdom. But any suggested set of examples will be contentious.

---

[1] Dr Samuel Johnson, 'Letter to Boswell' in J Boswell, *The Life of Samuel Johnson*, vol 3 (1791) 283.

I. The Virtue of Democracy (1): Failed Candidates

Why is democratic government embedded in western conventional wisdom? It is not as if there have been no reservations, or no scepticism. Winston Churchill's observation on 11 November 1947, in a debate in the House of Commons on what was to become the Parliament Act 1949, is very well known. He was then the Leader of the Opposition. He said:

> Many forms of Government have been tried, and will be tried in this world of sin and woe. No one pretends that democracy is perfect or all-wise. Indeed, it has been said that democracy is the worst form of Government except all those other forms that have been tried from time to time ...[2]

Churchill is also credited with the observation that 'the best argument against democracy is a five-minute conversation with the average voter', though the attribution has been disputed. Benjamin Franklin, the only man to sign the Declaration of Independence of 1776, the Treaty of Paris of 1783 and the United States Constitution of 1787, speaking of the last of these in his most famous speech, said 'I agree to this Constitution with all its faults'.[3]

This ambivalence about democracy has deep roots. Jacob Burckhardt, the great nineteenth-century historian of Greek culture, said:

> Culture [in ancient Greece] was to a high degree determined and dominated by the State, both in the positive and in the negative sense, since it demanded first and foremost of every man that he should be a citizen. Every individual felt that the *polis* lived in him. This supremacy of the *polis*, however, is fundamentally different from the supreme power of the modern State, which seeks only to keep its material hold on every individual, while the *polis* required of every man that he should serve it, and hence intervened in many concerns which are now left to individual and private judgment.[4]

Oswyn Murray, in his Introduction to the 1998 edition of Burckhardt,[5] cites this passage and comments:

> This attitude makes his [Burckhardt's] picture of Athenian democracy in particular unsympathetic: the ability of the demagogues to manipulate the masses becomes the most dangerous and most tyrannical form of political power that can be imagined. The prevalence of malicious and arbitrary prosecution by individual sycophants in a system where the law was the expression of the will of the people led to a permanent situation, like that which had existed temporarily during the reign of terror in the French Revolution, where the power to impose confiscation of property, dishonour, removal

---

[2] HC Deb 11 November 1947 vol 444 col 207.
[3] Benjamin Franklin, Speech to the Constitutional Convention, Philadelphia (17 September 1787).
[4] J Burckhardt, *The Greeks and Greek Civilisation*, ed O Murray, tr S Stern (Harper Collins, 1998).
[5] ibid.

of citizen rights, exile and death was absolute, and the individual had no rights at all against the will of the *demos*.[6]

Murray's observations, though cast in the context of ancient Greek politics, are highly pertinent to the imperative of the constitutional balance. '[T]he individual had no rights at all against the will of the *demos*': the avoidance of this political vice depends in the modern State upon the constitutional balance.

What, then, are the candidates for democracy's virtue? First, it may be said to promote or vindicate the idea of *self-determination*. But self-determination is a loose concept. It is perhaps most apt in the context of arguments about colonialism and empire, though even there it signals more often the beginning than the end of the debate, in situations (to take examples that relate to the United Kingdom) as diverse as the troubles of Northern Ireland, the defence of the Falkland Islands and Britain's relations with Spain concerning the British Overseas Territory of Gibraltar. I am not here concerned with such questions but with the merits of democracy as the means of internal government within a single State. In that context the idea of self-determination can only refer to a right of some kind in the hands of the individual citizen. So regarded, however, the notion of self-determination serves only to confuse. Whereas issues about the control by one State of a territory beyond its boundary may be illuminated by the claim that a *people* possess or should possess a right of self-determination, the proposition that *individual persons* should enjoy such a right, and for that reason democratic government must be vouchsafed to them, is altogether harder to understand.

More than this: it is merely fantasy, or at least hyperbole. To describe a quinquennial visit to the polling-booth as a vindication of the individual's right to self-determination is little more than hot air – all the more so if you consistently vote for the losing side. Democracy, direct or indirect, is essentially participatory. The citizen is subjected to the will of the majority, whether he or she likes it or not. That citizen may throughout his or her adult life vote for the losing party at every election, or always support policies that are rejected. Whether he or she does so or not, he or she takes part in the making of a communal choice. He or she does not vindicate or satisfy an *individual* right of self-determination.

Seen as such a right, then, self-determination cannot constitute a virtue of democracy.

But what about self-determination seen as the people's communal right to decide who should rule? Does this not give power and effect to *the will of the people*? Regular compulsory elections mean that government policy will reflect, however roughly and imperfectly, measures of which the people as a whole approve. There will not, or not for long, be too gross a separation between the will of the people and what the government imposes on them by enacted law or ministerial discretion. The sanction of the polling-booth is a voice at the government's shoulder,

---

[6] ibid xxxvi.

a telling whisper that if it makes laws that do not more or less appeal to the public – and so reflect the will of the people – it will be thrown from office.

This assumes, of course, that the 'will of the people' is itself an intelligible or realistic concept. I think that is at best doubtful. It is not unlike the idea of the intention of Parliament (to which I shall come in chapter 7): the attribution of a single state of mind to a many-headed body. From time to time, perhaps especially at times of national crisis (real or apparent), there may be a general sense, shared by a seeming or actual majority of the people, that the country should move in this direction or that. Or there may be a general revulsion against the propagation of an extreme political position. But these are fragile instances of the will of the people: they arise in exceptional (or what one hopes are exceptional) situations.

Writing in *The Times* on 15 March 2017 about populist and revolutionary political groups, Daniel Finkelstein (Lord Finkelstein) expressed himself more robustly:

> [P]opulist and revolutionary movements, whether violent or relatively benign, share a common idea and that idea is false. This false idea is that there is a voice of the people and a simple way of interpreting the voice of the people. From this first mistake flows [*sic*] all their other mistakes ... [T]hey die having never identified the voice of the people, because there isn't such a thing. There are many people, and they speak with many voices. The people live varied lives, and have varied interests, and have conflicting beliefs and competing rights.

In any event the relationship between 'the will of the people' (if there is such a thing) and action by the government is indirect, and from time to time thoroughly insecure. As everyone knows, governments do not always fulfil their promises made in the election campaign. Not because the promises were cynically made: sometimes events prohibit their fulfilment, sometimes the government has good reason to change its mind, sometimes the seas of office are much rougher than they looked from the harbour of opposition. Moreover, it is, in the United Kingdom at least, received constitutional doctrine that members of Parliament are their electors' representatives, not their delegates. Their duty is to act according to their conscience, not under any orders of their constituency.[7]

In any case the will of the people, in any sense in which you choose to use the term and however it is expressed, is no guarantee of good law or policy. The price of universal suffrage is that the vote of the stupid, malicious and ignorant elector (if he or she troubles to exercise it) is worth the same as anyone else's. This, I think, is why the opponents of prisoners' voting rights are mistaken: we deny the vote to children, but otherwise there is no restriction by reference to the capacity of the voter (though some graduates used to have two votes). (Until the post-war Attlee Government, some of our universities sent MPs to Westminster elected by

---

[7] Edmund Burke's speech to the electors of Bristol is the classic text on the subject. I cite it in section III of this chapter in the discussion on referendums.

members of the university whether or not they had a vote elsewhere. The practice was brought from Scotland when James VI inherited the English throne in 1603.)

Democracy – no guarantor of good law or policy – is fully capable of suppressing minorities and perpetrating injustices. In 406 BC, towards the end of the Peloponnesian War, the Athenians were victorious in a sea battle at Arginusae, to the south of Lesbos. But twenty-five Athenian ships had been lost, with their crews. A north wind, of the kind that still today blows very strong in those beautiful but unpredictable waters, had hindered any rescue. In Athens, still governed by its direct democracy, the eight commanders were blamed. In their turn they blamed the trierarchs, the captains of individual ships. Proceedings were brought against the generals. The Council of the Athenians, which prepared the case for trial before the Assembly of the people, had yielded to public anger and decided that they would all be tried together, on a single motion. That was contrary to the law: each was entitled to have his separate case judged on its merits. A motion was brought to challenge the procedure as invalid. The presiding committee had to decide whether to accept this motion, or to allow an immediate vote on a resolution to try all the generals together. They were intimidated by the people, the democratic voice. There were threats of impeachment and arrest. The presiding committee gave way. The eight generals were tried together on a single vote. They were condemned to death. Six were executed: they included the son of the great statesman, Pericles. The other two, as the historian Bury coyly puts it, 'had prudently kept out of the way'.[8] But the presiding committee had not been unanimous. Unanimity was not required for their ruling. One member, the philosopher Socrates, had stood out against the illegal and unjust procedure for which the people bayed, though he did so in vain. Afterwards the Athenians repented. They knew that what had been done was illegal.[9] Socrates had been right; though when, seven years later, he reminded his own accusers of the fact, it did not save him from sentence of death. Democrats, no doubt, do not like to be reminded of democracy's failings.

But maybe democracy has another virtue: it promotes *equality*. The universal suffrage is an equaliser in the obvious sense that everyone enjoys it; though if you consistently vote for the losing side, I doubt if you would feel very equal. There is no other sense in which democracy promotes equality. Consider these various categories of equality. There is economic equality, or at least a bias in its favour. There is equality of opportunity or access, particularly in the fields of education, health and work. There is equality before the law. Others may be suggested or asserted, such as equality of access to a clean environment, or equality of treatment

---

[8] Bury citation t/c.

[9] Or at least some of them did. Sir Kenneth Dover says (*Greek Popular Morality* (Blackwell, 1974) 158, fn 17), 'When Socrates resisted the pressure of the assembly to put to the vote the proposal that the generals should be tried together after the battle of Arginoussai (Xen. *Hell.* I. 7.15), he acted with exemplary courage, but he was not giving precedence to conscience over law; many people at the time, and most people after the event, thought that the proposal was illegal.'

as between persons of different sexual orientation. Some of equality's potential categories run into one another. None of them, however, is settled by an appeal to democracy. Some – equality before the law, equality of treatment – are functions of our foundational principles, not least that of fairness. But the laws that democracy may enact bear no necessary relationship to the actual or putative merits of any of these claims. Any one of them may be more or less popular, practical or politically expedient. Democratic law has no necessary moral content. It may perpetrate gross inequalities.

Equality is anyway a tricky business.[10] It is too often confused with the ideal of fairness.

II. The Virtue of Democracy (2): Its True Virtue

What then *is* democracy's virtue? Without democracy the government is by definition autocratic. Democracy is a necessary brake on the engine of public power. It is an antidote against tyranny. Here is its true virtue. The sanction of the polling-booth provides a corrective medicine: albeit, perhaps, more of an emetic than an antidote. The electorate can throw out the government. Albert Camus, in *The Rebel*, said that democracy is more important for what it prevents than for what it allows.

However, democracy's negative virtue – the prevention of tyranny – has a positive aspect, closely linked to the prevention of tyranny. The good constitution must allow for difference and disputation; in short, for pluralism. I said in the Introduction that it is an inherent feature of unruly humankind that what benefits the people will always be contentious. Democracy promotes pluralism, because it forces government to listen to contrary voices, and may throw it out of power if it fails to listen hard enough (and sometimes, of course, even if it does). The force of contrary voices makes democracy hostile to the command theory of morals.

Even so, as I have said, it is no guarantor of good law or policy. Like the Roman god Janus, democracy has two faces: its virtue is as a prophylactic against tyranny, but its vice is its openness to short-term, populist measures (or sometimes worse). But there is more. Democracy's virtue as an antidote to tyranny means that the electorate has no moral authority – and should have no legal authority – to deprive their successors of this same antidote. It calls to mind the wisdom of Edmund Burke, who believed that the social order involves

---

[10] Henry Becque said, 'What makes equality such a difficult business is that we only want it with our superiors' (*Querelles literaires*, 1890). Note also L Trilling, *The Liberal Imagination: Essays on Literature and Society* (Secker and Warburg, 1951): 'We who are liberal and progressive know that the poor are our equals in every sense except that of being equal to us.'

a partnership between the living, the dead and the yet unborn.[11] And the right of later generations to democracy's protection against tyranny gives moral strength to the constitutional truth that Parliament cannot bind its successors. (Parliament '[b]eing sovereign ... cannot abandon its sovereignty'.[12]) It is interesting that the abolition effected by the Parliament Act 1911 of the power of the House of Lords to reject prospective legislation passed by the Commons, so as to define the authority of the Upper House as a delaying function only, has by section 2(1) of the 1911 Act no application to a Bill containing any provision to extend the maximum duration of Parliament beyond five years. Were such a Bill to come before it, the House of Lords would enjoy all the powers it had before 1911. In this respect the unelected peers are democracy's guardians of last resort.

But democracy's virtue as an antidote to tyranny amounts to much more than an obligation to preserve itself for the future. It marks a vital connection between democratic government on the one hand and on the other the judicial review jurisdiction, and therefore our foundational principles of reason, fairness and the presumption of liberty. The nature of democracy's virtue effects an important reconciliation between the claims to supreme power of the elected branch of government and the constraints upon that same power imposed by the foundational principles. It is because the virtue of tyranny's avoidance – democracy's virtue – demands not only that the polling-booth remain effective. It means also that if elected government chooses to make law that is arbitrary and capricious, it stifles its own justification: for arbitrary, capricious law by definition tends towards tyranny; the democracy itself becomes tyrannous. The foundational principles are the constitution's prophylactic against arbitrary, capricious law. Accordingly they – and therefore the Rule of Law – are not the enemies of democratic government. Although, as I said in the Introduction, democracy and the Rule of Law are not natural bedfellows, still, the foundational principles that give life to the Rule of Law are the very guardians of democracy's integrity. Democratic government, then, lends itself to the Rule of Law. The two of them may be inclined to resent each other, but the ballot-box warns the ruler to make space for the power of independent adjudication and hence for the law's foundational principles; and the authority of the popular vote warns the unelected judicial guardians of the constitution not to press their exuberance too far. They work in effective harmony only through the medium of the constitutional balance.

If democracy's virtue is, as I have suggested, as an antidote to tyranny, then it may be said to rest in the *framework* democratic government provides for the exercise of State power, rather than the quality of a democratic State's decisions. The framework metaphor is useful, because it begins to focus the constitutional

---

[11] E Burke, *Reflections on the Revolution in France*, ed LG Mitchell (Oxford University Press, 1993).

[12] Para 59 of my judgment in *Thoburn v Sunderland City Council* [2002] EWHC 195 (Admin), [2003] QB 151.

balance. It gives us the question, how big should the framework be? What is the legitimate scope of democratic government? What (if any) are or ought to be the substantive limits upon democratic power? These questions bring us directly to the reach and force of the foundational principles.

Before coming to that, it is useful just to say this. The foundational principles of reason, fairness and the presumption of liberty are manifestly not set in stone. Not only is their scope, their reach, endlessly contentious. They mark the very points where democratic and judicial power are liable to disagree. They are the questions whose answers define the edge, the limit, of the power that statute gives to government. The independent judge will always seek to find the edge, and do so without bias. But very obviously government itself will have much to say about where the edge falls. The distinct approaches of courts and government to the settlement of this boundary is informed by their respective moralities, Kantian and utilitarian, to which I shall turn in the next chapter.

I shall next discuss a political force that may disrupt the constitutional balance, and distort the relative powers of courts and governments. I do so to illustrate an important truth: that we should not be complacent about the security of the constitutional balance. The political force in question is the institution of the referendum.

III. Referendums

In 2014 there was a referendum in Scotland about whether that country should become an independent State; in 2016 another, in the United Kingdom, about whether we should leave the European Union – Brexit.[13] The voters said No to the first, Yes to the second. I have nothing to say (at least not here) about the merits of either issue (nor of the fact that it seems to me profoundly undemocratic that in 2014 only those resident in Scotland, and not the inhabitants of England, Wales or Northern Ireland, were allowed to vote on the prospective dissolution of the United Kingdom). I am concerned with the use in principle of a referendum to obtain the opinion of the people – generally in response to a simplistic question – upon an issue of great constitutional significance. This is important, because the result of such a referendum appears to constitute a source of democratic power that challenges the democratic power of Parliament. It thus produces two democratic poles, one representative, one direct, in opposition to each other. This may destabilise the constitutional balance, and therefore, ultimately, the efficacy of the Rule of Law.

---

[13] Professor David Feldman and Veronika Fikfak presented a detailed paper (D Feldman and V Fikfak, 'The Constitutional Impact of National Referendums and the UK's Secession from the EU' (2019) 31(1) *European Review of Public Law* 139) dealing with the ramifications of the 2016 referendum, to the annual conference of the European Public Law Organisation in September 2018.

The moral force – if that is what it should be called – of the Brexit referendum result did two things. First, as I have suggested, it generated a source of democratic authority to rival that of Parliament. But secondly, and this is closely related, it distorted the nature of the duty of a Member of Parliament. In 1774 Edmund Burke made a speech to the electors of Bristol. He said this:

> [I]t ought to be the happiness and glory of a representative to live in the strictest union, the closest correspondence, and the most unreserved communication with his constituents. Their wishes ought to have great weight with him; their opinion, high respect; their business, unremitted attention. It is his duty to sacrifice his repose, his pleasures, his satisfactions, to theirs; and above all, ever, and in all cases, to prefer their interest to his own. But his unbiased opinion, his mature judgment, his enlightened conscience, he ought not to sacrifice to you, to any man, or to any set of men living. These he does not derive from your pleasure; no, nor from the law and the constitution. They are a trust from Providence, for the abuse of which he is deeply answerable. Your representative owes you, not his industry only, but his judgment; and he betrays, instead of serving you, if he sacrifices it to your opinion.[14]

It seems clear that a majority of the Members of the House of Commons were in fact opposed to Brexit. It is true that during the referendum campaign the Government distributed a leaflet stating that '[t]he government will implement what you decide', thus creating a moral commitment (though none was contained in the European Union Referendum Act 2015, which authorised the referendum). Many parliamentarians, in lending their support to what became the European Union (Notification of Withdrawal) Act 2017, voted to give effect to what was regarded as an imperative mandate from the people, expressed in the referendum result, and not in accordance with their own mature judgement on the EU issue. It is notable that on *Question Time* on the BBC on the day of the Act's Royal Assent, 16 March 2017, the Conservative MP Jacob Rees-Mogg (a constitutionalist, one would have thought, if ever there was one) stated that 'the fundamental point is the referendum was authoritative'. Was it? Not by reference to any established constitutional principle. It is interesting also that the leading article in the *Sunday Telegraph* on 4 December 2016 – the day before the Article 50 hearing in the Supreme Court began[15] – made the point, '[t]he judges are being asked to rule on whether the Brexit-backing voters or Remain-backing MPs should have greater authority'. Lord Patten, speaking in the House of Lords in January 2018, called referendums 'a sin against parliamentary democracy'. Writing in *The Times* (6 March 2018), Rachel Sylvester quotes a senior Conservative: 'Probably 80 per cent of Tory MPs, and the majority of ministers, don't think Brexit is in the national interest but they feel gagged by the referendum.'

---

[14] Edmund Burke, Speech to the Electors of Bristol, 3 November 1774, in *The Works of the Right Honourable Edmund Burke*, vol 1 (Henry G Bohn, 1854–56) ch 13, doc 7, available at https://press-pubs.uchicago.edu/founders/documents/v1ch13s7.html.
[15] *Miller v Secretary of State* [2017] UKSC 5.

The MPs faced a dilemma: between loyalty to Burke's principle and loyalty to the referendum result. They have chosen the latter. The opposition of two democratic poles poses a real constitutional difficulty.

One might suppose that the institution of party whips in Parliament, which day to day constrains the voting choices of MPs, has in any case weakened the force of Burke's appeal to the elected representative's individual conscience and judgement. That may be so, but the power of the whips is at least an aspect of Parliament's own procedures. In contrast, the moral pressure of the referendum result has undermined the integrity of representative democracy from the outside.

And it has generated a new realm of controversy for the courts. The judges of the Divisional Court were vilified for their decision in November 2016 that the initiation of the procedure provided by Article 50 of the Lisbon Treaty required Parliamentary authority. The *Daily Mail* headline on 4 November, apparently penned by the political editor, James Slack, screamed 'Enemies of the People'. It seems a pity that a national newspaper such as the *Daily Mail* appears to be ignorant of the difference between abuse and criticism. The *Independent* (perhaps gleefully) reported that the publication in the *Mail* had so far sparked 1,108 complaints to the Independent Press Standards Organisation. The *Daily Telegraph* was hardly any better than the *Mail*: its headline was 'The judges versus the people'. After the attacks on the Divisional Court, eighteen law professors from the universities of Oxford and Cambridge wrote to *The Times*.[16] They said of the Press assaults that they '[show] an indifference to the essential conditions for the rule of law which is objectionable and deeply worrying'.

What clearly excited the *Mail* and some of the newspapers – and, to their shame, some of the politicians – was the perception that the decision was an affront to the sacred voice of the people. Such a rollercoaster view of democracy is no companion of the Rule of Law. The professors' letter to *The Times* also '[deplored] the failure of the government (and in particular, of the Lord Chancellor) to condemn [the reports]'. The Prime Minister's response to the newspaper reports was delayed, feeble and muted. It demonstrated an abject failure to understand her own constitutional role.

The force of a referendum result may, as I have said, disrupt or destabilise the constitutional balance because it is liable to be expressed without nuance: Yes or No. The question will have been simplistic and the answer black or white. The constitutional balance needs a broader canvas. That said, I would accept that Burke's principle is not the beginning and end of responsible democratic politics. Despite the stresses and strains, there may be a proper place – a strictly limited place – for referendums in our constitutional arrangements. Whether there is or not engages questions that travel beyond the scope of these lectures. Professor Vernon Bogdanor has said in the *Financial Times* that '[i]t is a weakness in the

---

[16] *The Times* (9 November 2016).

doctrine of parliamentary sovereignty that some decisions are so fundamental that a decision by parliament alone does not yield legitimacy for them'.[17] The referendum on Scottish independence in 2014 was perhaps an example. Whether the same can be said of the Brexit referendum may be much more doubtful. My point is only that a second, populist centre of gravity for democracy poses dangers to the constitutional balance – to the relationship between government and the courts, and therefore to the Rule of Law.

IV. Conclusion – Restraint

The efficacy of democratic government, and of the constitutional balance, depends in the end on more than wise legal arrangements. It depends on the patient virtue of governmental restraint. We would do well to remember what was said by Lord Moulton, sometime law lord and government minister, in 1912:

> It is the fundamental principle of Democracies to bow to the decision of the majority. But in accepting this we do not surrender ourselves to the rule of the majority in all things, but only in those things which are of a kind fit to be regulated by Government. We do not admit, for instance, the right of the majority to decide whom we should marry or what should be our religion. These are but types of a vast number of matters of great interest in life which we hold to be outside the decision of a majority, and which are for the individual alone to decide. But in form the power of our Government has no restrictions. It has the power to do everything, and too often it forgets that this limitless power does not leave the scope of its legislation a matter of absolute choice on its part, but a choice fettered by a duty to act according to the trust reposed in it, and to abstain from legislating in matters where legislation is not truly within its province. And what is true as to the scope of legislation is also true to a great extent as to the nature of that legislation. But there is a widespread tendency to regard the fact that they *can* do a thing as meaning that they *may* do it. There can be no more fatal error than this. Between 'can do' and 'may do' ought to exist the whole realm which recognises the sway of duty, fairness, sympathy, taste, and all the other things that make life beautiful and society possible. It is this confusion between 'can do' and 'may do' which made [Lord Moulton] fear at times lest in the future the worst tyrannies will be found in Democracies. Interests which are not strongly represented in Parliament may be treated as though they had no rights by Governments who think that the power and the will to legislate amount to a justification of that legislation. Such a principle would be death to liberty. No part of our life would be secure from interference from without. If [Lord Moulton] were asked to define tyranny, [he] would say it was yielding to the lust of governing. It is only when Governments feel it an honourable duty not to step beyond

that which was in reality and not only in form put into their hands that the world will know what true Freedom is.[18]

Our democracy in practice operates, of course, through the sovereignty of Parliament, which I shall discuss in chapter 8, where I shall have more to say about the relationship between the legislative power and our constitutional fundamentals.

---

[18] Address to the Authors' Club in London entitled 'Law and Manners' (4 November 1912). I am indebted to the late Sir Robin Day (as I am for much else besides) for the reference.

3

Two Moralities

In chapter 2 I said that the foundational principles of reason, fairness and the presumption of liberty are the constitution's prophylactic against tyranny in the form of arbitrary, capricious law; so that they – and therefore the Rule of Law – are the very guardians of democracy's integrity. Law and democracy to this extent are in the same camp; on the same side. Their relationship is conditioned by the constitutional balance. But what is reasonable, what is fair, above all what should be forbidden to the citizen and what should be allowed to the State (an antithesis at the core of the presumption of liberty: I shall have more to say about it in chapter 5), are endlessly contentious questions. Their answers define the edge, the limit, of the power that statute gives to the ruler.

The distinct approaches of courts and government to the settlement of this boundary are informed by their respective moralities: Kantian and utilitarian. The contrast between them underpins the constitutional balance. The distinction between these moralities is central to the relationship between judicial and political power, and therefore to a practical understanding of the constitutional balance, which mediates between them. They are the subject of this chapter.

I. The Nature of the Two Moralities

The Kantian morality of law is centred on the autonomy of every individual. The utilitarian morality of government is centred on the interests or well-being of the people as a whole. The Kantian morality of law, though sometimes it needs to be qualified, inheres in the notion that duties should be honoured and rights should be vindicated, whether or not the general welfare of the State and its citizens is thereby enhanced. The autonomy of every individual also dictates the need of fair procedure, and the Kantian morality of law is integral to the idea of justice. By contrast, the morality of government puts the general welfare of the State and its citizens centre stage: 'the greatest happiness of the greatest number'. Sometimes it too needs to be qualified. It is obvious that these two moralities may very readily be in conflict. Professor Vernon Bogdanor, in *The New British Constitution*,[1] recalls Sir Stephen Sedley's reference to 'a new and still emerging

---

[1] V Bogdanor, *The New British Constitution* (Hart Publishing, 2009) ch 3, 82.

paradigm [comprising] a bi-polar sovereignty of the Crown in Parliament and the Crown in the courts'. Bogdanor continues:

> The difficulty with such a paradigm, of course, is that the two poles of the new bi-polar sovereignty, far from collaborating in the sharing of authority, can all too easily come into conflict.[2]

Professor Bogdanor is plainly right. But the possibility – no, the certainty – of a degree of conflict is no reason to reject the model of two moralities. They are a signal of our developing constitution. In *International Transport Roth GmbH v Secretary of State* in 2003,[3] after referring to an observation of Iacobucci J in the Supreme Court of Canada,[4] I said this:

> 70. Not very long ago, the British system was one of parliamentary supremacy pure and simple. Then, the very assertion of constitutional rights as such would have been something of a misnomer, for there was in general no hierarchy of rights, no distinction between 'constitutional' and other rights. Every Act of Parliament had the same standing in law as every other, and so far as rights were given by judge-made law, they could offer no competition to the status of statutes. The courts evolved rules of interpretation which favoured the protection of certain basic freedoms, but in essence Parliament legislated uninhibited by claims of fundamental rights.
>
> 71. In its present state of evolution, the British system may be said to stand at an intermediate stage between parliamentary supremacy and constitutional supremacy, to use the language of the Canadian case. Parliament remains the sovereign legislature; there is no superior text to which it must defer ...; there is no statute which by law it cannot make. But at the same time, the common law has come to recognise and endorse the notion of constitutional, or fundamental rights. These are broadly the rights given expression in the European Convention on Human Rights and Fundamental Freedoms ..., but their recognition in the common law is autonomous ...

The language of constitutional rights is not the same as that of the two moralities. Nor is Sir Stephen's reference to a bi-polar sovereignty of the Crown in Parliament and the Crown in the courts. But all these formulations point to the core value of the constitutional balance.

The two moralities possess immediate and powerful echoes of Professor Ronald Dworkin's well-known distinction between principle and policy.[5] More generally they exemplify two major and very familiar post-Enlightenment traditions of moral philosophy: the philosophy of duties and rights on the one hand, and the philosophy of utilitarianism on the other: Kant and Bentham. These traditions are intricate and difficult. There are, for example, many problems with the idea of Kant's categorical imperative, one version of which reads 'act only on that maxim which you can at the same time will that it should become a

---

[2] ibid.

[3] *International Transport Roth GmbH v Secretary of State for the Home Department* [2003] QB 728.

[4] In *Vriend v Alberta* [1998] SCR 493, 563.

[5] See, for example, R Dworkin, *Law's Empire* (Hart Publishing, 1998) 221–24, 243–44, 310–12, 338–39, 381.

universal law'[6] – not exactly a rallying-cry to the moral barricades. And the associated idea that every person is to be treated as an end and not a means is only telling if it is heavily qualified. We treat shopkeepers and professors as means to ends – in one case the acquisition of goods, in the other the acquisition of learning; but they (and other suppliers) are, or should be, decently rewarded. The real principle is that you should not *exploit* other people.

Utilitarianism is also beset by notorious problems leading to theoretical adjustments and the wobble between what is called rule-utilitarianism and act-utilitarianism.

One reason why, in elaborating these opposing theories, the philosophers have faced formidable difficulties is their insistent quest for the Holy Grail of uniformity – the search for a single moral theory that can be shown to be correct for all cases. Thus in his major work *On What Matters*, acknowledged as a philosophical contribution of great importance,[7] Derek Parfit sought to synthesise the three major normative traditions of Kantianism, contractualism and consequentialism (of which utilitarianism is a variety) into a unified whole, which he called 'Triple Theory'.[8] However, since I do not propose to follow the quest for the Sangreal of uniformity, I need say nothing about the conceptual challenges encountered by those who do. It is enough for my deployment of the two political moralities to recognise the practical contrast between the two values to which they give substance, the autonomy of every individual and the interests of the people as a whole. Whatever the problems of either as an all-embracing moral theory, as distinctive values they are perfectly coherent and the contrast between them, though not absolute, is perfectly real.

The constitutional balance requires that the two moralities are so far as possible in harmony; each of them served to the least prejudice of the other. The tenor of our constitution, the relationship between the ruler and the ruled, is given by the relative weight our law accords to each. I should explain the contrast between them, and therefore the nature of each of them, more closely. Consider these overlapping points.

A. The Natural Provinces of Courts and Government

First, it must already be apparent that whereas the autonomy of every individual is a function of justice and therefore the natural province of the courts, the well-being of the people as a whole is a function of democratic government and therefore the natural province of the politicians. They may and do trespass into

---

[6] Derek Parfit suggests that a revised version – 'Everyone ought to follow the principles whose universal acceptance everyone could rationally will' – 'might be what Kant was trying to find: the supreme principle of morality': D Parfit, *On What Matters* (Oxford University Press, 2011) ch 14, 342.

[7] See, for example, Peter Singer's review in the *Times Literary Supplement* (20 May 2011). Derek Parfit died on 1 January 2017.

[8] Parfit (n 6) ch 17, 411–17.

each other's territory (and I shall have more to say about that), but this allocation of space between them is the paradigm.

B. The Two Philosophies are Apt to their Respective Spheres

It is therefore no coincidence that the courts' natural territory is marked, broadly at least, by a Kantian philosophy and that of government by a utilitarian philosophy. The administration of justice is necessarily concerned with the adjudication of duties and rights in the particular case according to established rules and principles. The systematic application of a utilitarian philosophy would be inconsistent with this adjudicative function. It would require the judges to be prepared, if they thought it in the public interest, to set aside applicable law in the name of some perceived greater good. But that would be a denial of justice; it would be a denial of law.

Politicians, governments, are by necessity utilitarians. It is because their primary task is to judge, not settled rights and duties, but conflicting, and often strategic, *interests* – between hospitals and schools, between social security and defence, between the opposing claims of high tax and low tax policies. In short, their primary focus is on outcomes. Utilitarianism is necessarily and honourably the moral language of government. Rights and duties are necessarily and honourably the moral language of justice and therefore of law. This distinction is at the core of the constitutional balance.

C. The Methods of Courts and Government are Suited to their Respective Moralities

These contrasting moralities reflect the contrasting *methods* of Parliament and the courts. Their respective methods are suited to their respective moralities. This is of particular importance for the relation between judicial review and the Rule of Law. I shall describe the methods of the common law and of the legislature in the next chapter. It is enough for present purposes to give a postage-stamp summary. The common law is gradual and evolutive, but legislation is immediate. It can only make black-letter law. Unlike the common law, it can simply sweep away what has gone before. At a seminar in Cambridge on 19 January 2017, Sir Stephen Laws, First Parliamentary Counsel until 2012 (to whose critique of the *UNISON* case I referred in chapter 1),[9] said that the starting-point for drafting any legislation is a blank sheet of paper.[10]

---

[9] Sir Stephen Laws, 'Second Guessing Policy Choices: The rule of law after the Supreme Court's UNISON judgment' (Policy Exchange, 14 March 2018) available at https://policyexchange.org.uk/wp-content/uploads/2018/03/Second-guessing-policy-choices-2.pdf.

[10] That would not of course be so in a State with a written constitution, to which any new legislation would be subject. Nor is it true for amendments or consolidations; but new law is the paradigm.

The result is that the Kantian morality of law is given effect through settled principles, but the utilitarian morality of government is not. This is why the respective methods of law and government are suited to their respective moralities. Law is nothing without principles, for without them its outcomes are only the bare choices of the judge, and that is not law but merely power. The common law's methodology is wholly apt to the development of principle. But no such principles are integral to the morality of government. As I said earlier, what is in the general interest of the people will always be contentious, and the rival contentions cannot be reduced to or derived from settled principles that are held in common by all factions. Parliament's method is wholly apt to the establishment of political outcomes.

I do not of course suggest that the process of government is generally unprincipled in some pejorative sense. It may be constrained, and shaped, by many factors: the ballot-box, the party machine, Parliamentary arithmetic, external circumstances, public opinion and the sheer political commitment of its actors. Political opponents will have their own strongly held political principles; but these are, necessarily and rightly, partisan, and may be volatile. They are not held in common as a shared heritage – far from it. The principles of left and right are (generally) in muscular opposition to each other. Where political disagreement is more complicated than a single unbridgeable chasm, factional differences, though they may be more nuanced, are just as tightly gripped. There are, of course, important qualities that straddle the political divide: apart from honesty and a commitment to democratic process, they include a presumption of goodwill, firmness of purpose and an aspiration of competence. But unlike our foundational principles of reason, fairness and the presumption of liberty, these are not principles that directly condition the merits of decisions. They are characteristics of honourable decision-makers.

For these reasons the morality of government is much more open-ended than the morality of law; and law is a much tamer beast than government. The core principles of the morality of law – reason, fairness and the presumption of liberty – are by their nature bound to condition the administration of individual rights and duties very closely, and to that extent direct the outcome of judicial decisions. But the primary qualities of the morality of government – goodwill, firmness of purpose and competence – though vital, have only a strategic influence on the outcome of government activity, the construction of policy.

We can see, then, that the evolutive nature of the common law's methods is apt to the development and application of the principles that give effect to the law's Kantian morality; and the immediacy of Parliament's method, the making of black-letter law, is apt to the achievement of government's utilitarian outcomes; but it is, at the same time, fundamentally unsuited to the evolution of constitutional principles.

D. The Two Moralities and the Constitutional Balance

The constitutional balance is illuminated by these marriages of method and moral philosophy, of law and of government respectively. The constitution needs a balance between the two moralities, each having substantial weight in the distribution of State power. If one is all but expunged by the onward march of the other, the constitution is corrupted. Consider each extreme. First, the case where the morality of government has vastly greater force than the morality of law. In that case individual rights – the claims of justice – are liable to be crushed by the utilitarian imperatives of government. The 'elective dictatorship' of which Lord Hailsham famously spoke in his Richard Dimbleby Lecture in 1976[11] is inescapably enhanced. Now consider the converse case: the morality of law has vastly greater force than the morality of government. Then the general public interest is stifled: its voice unheard in the tumult of competing claims.

But there is a greater nightmare. What would a constitution be like if neither morality played any part in it? It would be no constitution at all, or none worth the name. If there were anything called law, it would lack all principle. If there were anything called government, its rule would be vicious and inhumane. What marks the most brutal kind of autocracy is its lack of both moralities. But if both play their part in the State, the constitutional balance is a necessity.

The morality of law, then, must not forget the impact of individual claims on the community; and the morality of government must not forget the impact of community claims on individuals. But it is not only that both moralities are needed for their own sake. They are also both needed because in each of the extreme cases the prevailing morality is corrupted by its own inherent weakness. What are these weaknesses? The weakness of the morality of government is the side-effect of democracy's virtue, its corrective medicine, the antidote it provides against tyranny: populism, the price of the polling-booth: the capacity of democracy to trample over justice in the name of a popular cause. Remember the aftermath of the battle of Arginusae.[12] But the morality of law, given practical effect by the institution of enforceable rights, has its weakness too. The great American jurist Oliver Wendell Holmes said, in a case in the US Supreme Court in 1908, that '[a]ll rights tend to declare themselves absolute to their logical extreme'.[13] And this is surely true. It is in the nature of rights that given an inch, they claim a mile.

---

[11] The phrase is found a century earlier, in describing Giuseppe Garibaldi's doctrines, and was used by Hailsham in lectures in 1968 and 1969. It is right to say that Lord Hailsham was referring to the state in which Parliament is dominated by the government of the day, rather than the subjection of law to democratic rule.

[12] See ch 2, section I.

[13] *Hudson County Water Co v McCarter* 209 US 349, 355 (1908).

Each of these weaknesses will be at its strongest when the morality to which it belongs is decisively in the ascendant. But government restrains law, and law restrains government. Popular pressure tends to put a brake on overweening claims of right; and the justice of individual causes tends to put a brake on measures fuelled by populist excess. And so the constitutional balance needs both moralities, for their own sake and also because each mitigates the other's weakness.

The balance is bound to vary under the influence of circumstance. In times of national danger the morality of government will, rightly, have a louder voice. But still, a balance must be struck; the tension between the demands of security and the claims of justice and rights is necessary as well as familiar.[14] More generally, the balance will differ from State to State, tending this way or that under the influence of distinctive cultural and political traditions. There is not a universal ideal, a single perfect striking of the balance to which every State should aspire. There is no Platonic Form for a constitution. This has a particular significance here in Europe. This differential allocation of the two political moralities from one State to another, this variation among constitutions, is what in truth justifies and requires the Strasbourg doctrine of the margin of appreciation, where the writ of the European Court of Human Rights runs.[15] More broadly, it should make us suspicious of aspirations to international government, the dream of some European politicians.[16]

II. Trespass

I said earlier that courts and government trespass into each other's natural territory. We should not, however, lose sight of the fact that the relation between the morality of law and the morality of government is complicated in practice. It reflects the fact that the Rule of Law has to live in the practical world, and the practical world has rough edges. It is inevitable that the two competing moralities jostle for position; inevitable, also, that there should be some cross-over between them. Thus the Kantian morality of the law may be modified by utilitarian considerations. The use of special advocates and closed hearings, where that is required on security grounds, is a compromise of the principle of open or public justice, justified on a plainly utilitarian basis. There are other, broader examples. The administration of justice needs procedural rules that in practical terms can only

---

[14] See, amongst many discussions, A Barak, *Human Rights and their Limitations: The Role of Proportionality*, FLJS Annual Lecture in Law and Society, Rhodes House, Oxford (4 June 2009), available at https://www.youtube.com/watch?v=tWNCusRTzeY; and A Barak, *Proportionality: Constitutional Rights and the Limitations* (Cambridge University Press, 2012).

[15] Lord Sumption thinks that the doctrine of the margin of appreciation has been shrunk by the Strasbourg Court 'to almost nothing': J Sumption QC, *Judicial and Political Decision-making: The Uncertain Boundary*, FA Mann Lecture 2011.

[16] Which is – I hope obviously – not to say that we should have reservations about the civilising benefits of developments of public international law.

be provided by statutory regulation, and which will often have a utilitarian, public interest overlay. The Limitation Acts are a good example: setting limits to the time in which proceedings may be brought may be seen as a function of justice – justice delayed is justice denied – but it is also in the general interest. It may save public money and (in a case with public ramifications) assuage public uncertainty. These are utilitarian considerations. Legislation, moreover, is needed from time to time to make sea changes in substantive legal provisions that are in general beyond the territory of the Kantian morality of the law.

A. Criminal Law

The law of crime yields starker, perhaps clearer instances. The law's approach to the punishment of criminals, in recent years at least, has involved an uneasy combination of philosophies. Retributive justice is one element. This is firmly in the Kantian camp: it means, to oversimplify, that the criminal gets what he or she deserves – no less but also (which is just as important) no more. Deterrence is another. This is firmly in the utilitarian camp: if we were only concerned with deterrence, as opposed to fitting the punishment to the crime, we might pass very heavy sentences for riding a bicycle without lights. There is, moreover, a deeper sense in which criminal punishment takes hold of the two moralities. The first measure of punishment is the degree of blameworthiness involved on the criminal's part. But the severity of punishment may also be affected by factors in the case the criminal did not intend and could not reasonably have foreseen. A drunk man, outside the pub, may quarrel with his equally drunk friend and punch him – once only: the friend falls, cracks his head on a kerbstone, suffers a subdural haemorrhage and dies. The defendant is prosecuted for manslaughter, instead of common assault, and is punished accordingly. Such a case raises difficult questions about the concept of responsibility that are beyond the scope of these observations. But to an extent at least the criminal has been punished beyond his deserts, and on prudential or public interest grounds. My point is only that outcomes like this involve both Kantian and utilitarian elements. A clearer instance, perhaps, was the sentence of imprisonment for public protection (IPP), introduced by the Criminal Justice Act 2003 (with effect from 2005) for certain classes of serious crime, and abolished in 2012. This was an indefinite sentence (though not a life sentence). The trial judge was required to fix a minimum term to serve the needs of retribution and deterrence, after whose expiry the criminal might apply to the Parole Board, which would order his or her release only if it concluded that he or she was no longer a danger to the public. Thus the minimum term served both a Kantian purpose – just deserts; and a utilitarian one – deterrence. Confinement thereafter was wholly utilitarian: the protection of the public. There is perhaps an irony in the fact that calls for the abolition of IPPs were largely based on what was primarily a Kantian consideration, namely that the prisons lacked the resources to provide sufficient rehabilitative courses to equip prisoners to persuade the Parole

Board that they were safe to release; and this was seen as unjust, since the prisoner would have served the term required for retribution and deterrence.[17]

The law of crime, then, provides a striking instance of a field that raises issues both of individual justice and of the public interest, and mingles the two moralities. I think it is interesting for present purposes because it displays a tension between the two moralities that is similar to a tension encountered in the public law field, especially that of human rights (which I shall discuss in greater detail in chapter 9). A plain example in that area concerns the deportation of foreign criminals: should the clear statutory policy of removing such criminals from the United Kingdom prevail over their family life with their children born in this jurisdiction? The case exemplifies the obvious fact that in a dispute between citizen and State, the interest asserted by the State will necessarily be a claim of public interest: and very often, though not always, a claim whose nature is utilitarian or consequentialist.

B. Trespass by Government

Sometimes, however, courts and government trespass into each other's natural territory without sufficient cause. I should emphasise (though it is obvious) that trespass is the wrong word for a case involving no more than a proportionate adjudication of a necessary clash between private right and public interest: that is the court's proper task where such a clash arises in the interpretation or application of statute (notably the human rights legislation). But there are cases where trespass is the right word – trespass by government and courts into each other's territory. I shall describe this kind of case. First, trespass by government.

The instance of government trespass into law's domain that is most relevant for our purpose consists in the case of legislation seeking to restrict or diminish the scope or effectiveness of the judicial review jurisdiction. Ouster clauses, such as that found in *Anisminic v Foreign Compensation Commission*,[18] are the most obvious example, but the courts have been able to curtail their reach by plumbing the resources of statutory construction. I shall return to *Anisminic* in the next chapter. A more sinister invasion is to be found in section 84 of the Criminal Justice and Courts Act 2015, which inserts new subsections into section 31 of the Senior Courts Act 1981 as follows:

(2A)   The High Court—

(a)   must refuse to grant relief on an application for judicial review …

if it appears to the court to be highly likely that the outcome for the applicant would not have been substantially different if the conduct complained of had not occurred.

---

[17] The complexities of the relationship between retribution, deterrence and indeed the rights of the criminal in the context of the courts' treatment of the most serious instances of the crime of murder are very valuably discussed in G Wansell, *Lifers* (Michael Joseph, 2016).
[18] *Anisminic v Foreign Compensation Commission* [1969] 2 AC 147.

(2B)   The court may disregard the requirements in subsection (2A)(a) ... if it considers that it is appropriate to do so for reasons of exceptional public interest.

(2C)   If the court grants relief ... in reliance on subsection (2B), the court must certify that the condition in subsection (2B) is satisfied.

There follow parallel provisions applying the same regime to the permission stage in judicial review proceedings.

I would draw attention to two linked features of this provision. First, it means that there will be cases in which an individual has been adversely affected, in his or her person or property, by an unlawful decision, but has no remedy: because it is 'highly likely' that the result would have been the same had the decision been lawfully made. That, surely, is an affront to the Rule of Law. The judicial review court possesses a discretion to refuse relief even if the claimant has a good legal point, and is likely to do so if it perceives the litigation as in reality pointless. But this statutory measure, subject to the 'exceptional public interest' provision in section 31(2B), takes that decision out of the judge's hands. The scope of the judicial power to vindicate the law's foundational principles is thus significantly diminished. Here, then, is a stark example of trespass by government – of government's utilitarian ethic – onto the field of the law. The government has taken over the role of the court, by confining the circumstances in which relief may be given in a judicial review case. The measure could only be justified on the footing that the judges are not to be trusted to find such limits for themselves.

But the second objectionable feature of this assault on the Rule of Law is much worse. It is sought to be justified by an out-and-out appeal to utilitarian considerations: so long as the outcome would have been the same anyway, no harm is done, and a lot of vexation and expense avoided. This consequential-ist approach minimises society's vital interest in seeing that public decisions are taken according to law. The affront to the Rule of Law is much greater than a mere mistrust of the judges' capacity to exercise their discretion properly. Due process is sacrificed. The protection of the law is significantly undermined. Officials responsible for public decisions may well come to think that so long as they get the result right, compliance with the law's discipline may take something of a back seat. There must be a real question as to whether the excepting provision in section 31(2B) – '[t]he court may disregard [the requirement to refuse relief] if it considers that it is appropriate to do so for reasons of exceptional public interest' – offers anything like a sufficient safeguard. It puts the courts in a very difficult position. The language of section 31(2B) makes it entirely plain that the disregard is only to be applied exceptionally. But any case in which an unlawful act is to be excused is surely to be considered exceptional. The courts must either stretch the subsection until it snaps, or kow-tow to an impoverished and cynical view of the Rule of Law.

I shall give one other instance of government trespass into law's domain. It concerns the law of defamation rather than judicial review. By section 40 of the Crime and Courts Act 2013, if it is brought into force, a newspaper not signed up to a State-approved regulator (the prospective regulator is called Impress) will be exposed to a high risk of an adverse order for costs in privacy and libel cases even if the newspaper wins the case. The purpose is to put pressure on the Press to submit to State-approved regulation. The chosen method is a strict curtailment of the courts' power and duty to make just orders for costs.

C. Trespass by Courts

What about trespass by the courts onto the territory of government? Because of the common law's evolutive method in comparison with Parliament's black-letter lawmaking, its trespasses are less clear cut than those of government. In a judicial review case concerning the use of discretionary power under statute, they happen when the courts, usually on the springboard of proportionality, pay insufficient respect to the margin of discretion the government decision-maker enjoys. The judges' acknowledgement of such a margin of discretion has often been referred to as judicial deference. This is an important idea, because it is one of the ways in which the courts articulate the limit or edge of governmental statutory power; and as we have seen, that is an exercise that is critical to the Rule of Law's effectiveness.

Judicial deference, to which I shall come in chapter 6, marks the space the law must give to the democratic power. As I have said, government must respect the Kantian morality of the law; so also the law must respect the utilitarian morality of government: this is the constitutional balance. I have focused on the Kantian morality of the law; but it is important not to marginalise the utilitarian morality of government. The two moralities represent the twin values of civilised government: the Rule of Law and the democratic power.

III. Justice

I said at the outset of this chapter that the Kantian morality of the law is integral to the idea of justice. One may of course multiply examples of the Kantian ethic of justice. But the best example of all – at least a very good one – is Lord Atkin's dissent in *Liversidge v Anderson*.[19] This case, decided by the House of Lords in 1941, concerned the Defence Regulations. The Regulations permitted the Minister to order the detention of any person if he had 'reasonable cause to believe', in effect, that the person constituted a danger to the defence of the realm. The Home Secretary ordered that Mr Liversidge be detained. Mr Liversidge sued. The Minister pleaded the Regulations. He declined to give particulars of his

---

[19] *Liversidge v Anderson* [1942] AC 206.

'reasonable belief', submitting that his mere assertion of it was enough. Four Law Lords agreed with him. Lord Atkin did not. He said:

> I view with apprehension the attitude of judges who on a mere question of construction when face to face with claims involving the liberty of the subject show themselves more executive minded than the executive. Their function is to give words their natural meaning, not, perhaps, in war time leaning towards liberty, but following the dictum of Pollock CB ... 'In a case in which the liberty of the subject is concerned, we cannot go beyond the natural construction of the statute.' In this country, amid the clash of arms, the laws are not silent. They may be changed, but they speak the same language in war as in peace. It has always been one of the pillars of freedom, one of the principles of liberty for which on recent authority we are now fighting, that the judges are no respecters of persons and stand between the subject and any attempted encroachments on his liberty by the executive, alert to see that any coercive action is justified in law. In this case I have listened to arguments which might have been addressed acceptably to the Court of King's Bench in the time of Charles I.[20]

The exercise by which the court turns principle into case law is at every turn informed by non-utilitarian considerations of justice. Principles of reason, fairness and the presumption of liberty, which I shall discuss more fully in chapter 5, are at work in practice. But there is an important *caveat*: as we shall see in particular in the discussion of fairness in chapter 5, utilitarian considerations may qualify the purity of the law's objective standards. Nothing is ever as simple as it seems.

IV. Postscript

Finally (for the time being) there is this to say about the two moralities. Some intrusion by one into the field of the other, as I have shown, is justified and indeed inevitable. But the greater the intrusion of either, the harder it is to justify. The constitutional balance, if it is respected, should prevent this. But it has to be worked at, defended, preserved. Politicians, judges, commentators need to understand this.

---

[20] ibid 244.

4

The Common Law

In this chapter I shall first describe the common law's place in our constitution, and especially its relation with statute law, the law of Parliament; and then I shall describe the methods of the common law. These are the medium through which the constitutional balance operates in this jurisdiction. First, a word about the nature of constitutions in general.

I. Constitutions

The term 'constitution' means, at least, that set of laws that in a sovereign State establish the relationship between the ruler and the ruled. Law in one form or another is therefore a defining element of every constitution, save in a territory where the people are ruled by the brute commands of whoever is the strongest leader from time to time; but we would deny the term 'constitution' to so coarse a state of affairs.

That is not to say that a constitution may not be autocratic yet still a constitution. But in any constitutional State the sovereign is always a body whose designation, as RTE Latham put it in the 1940s, 'must include the statement of rules for the ascertainment of his will, and those rules, since their observance is a condition of the validity of his legislation, are rules of law logically prior to him'.[1] The laws of the constitution will also contain definitions of the powers and duties of the sovereign: and the nature and exercise of these powers will mark the reach of individual freedom in the State.

Such laws make the constitution. This is true of every constitution, written or unwritten, exotic or familiar, common law or civilian. Law is the unifying principle of every constitution. Every constitution is made with a set of laws that (i) define the ruler, and in doing so establish the relationship between the ruler and the ruled, and (ii) contain definitions of the powers and duties of the sovereign. A constitution will also generally include (iii) principles for the proper exercise of the sovereign's powers and duties (and it is at this point, if anywhere, that the constitution is likely to cater for the protection of human rights).

These points matter for present purposes because the central place of law as the unifying principle of constitutional government underlines the vital importance of

---

[1] RTE Latham, *The Law and the Commonwealth* (Oxford University Press, 1949) 523, fn 4.

the quality of the foundational principles – reason, fairness and the presumption of liberty – which lift the law above the thin theory: the theory that says that the Rule of Law only requires that State power should be exercised in accordance with promulgated, non-retrospective law made according to established procedures. Those principles are at the heart of the Rule of Law, and integral to the constitutional balance. In our uncodified constitution they are generally shaped by the common law.

II. Statute Law

I should emphasise that in referring to the common law, I do not intend to connote only those free-standing principles of the law that stand quite apart from the interpretation of statutes. Statute law has of course itself provided important pillars in the constitutional edifice that are of the first importance: the Act of Union 1707, the legislation that confers and defines the franchise, and the devolution legislation: these go to (i) above: they describe the ruler. The Magna Carta of 1215, the Bill of Rights of 1689 and the European Communities Act 1972 go to (ii): they define, in part, the sovereign's powers and duties. It is important to note that the European Communities Act goes to (ii) rather than (i), for it means that at law there has been no transfer of State sovereignty from Westminster to Brussels. There is some discussion of that proposition in a judgment of mine in what has become known as the Metric Martyrs case;[2] and it is a fact not always appreciated in the course of the debates about Brexit. The Human Rights Act 1998 goes to (iii) (principles for the proper exercise of the sovereign's powers and duties).

What is the place of the common law in relation to principles that are gleaned from statute law? Every one of these constitutional statutes, and every other statute, is mediated to the people by the common law. An Act of Parliament is words on a page. Only the common law gives it life. It is a commonplace to say that the judges interpret legislation, and so they do. But, as I shall explain more fully, this is the opposite of an austere linguistic exercise. The construction of statutes, just as surely as the development of common law principles not touched by legislation, is the product of the common law's reason matured over time. The force of our constitution's provisions – (i), (ii) and (iii) above – is therefore delivered by the common law and its distinctive method. The unifying principle of our constitution is the common law.

It must be obvious that an Act of Parliament, words on a page, can have no effect without an interpreter. And the interpreter cannot be the lawmaker, the legislator, Parliament itself, and certainly not the executive. In *Cart & Ors*[3] in 2009 I said:

> 37. … The interpreter's role cannot be filled by the legislature or the executive: for in that case they or either of them would be judge in their own cause, with the ills of

---

[2] See my judgment in *Thoburn* [2003] QB 151.
[3] *R (on the application of Cart) v Upper Tribunal* [2009] EWHC Admin 3052, [2010] 2 WLR 1012.

arbitrary government which that would entail. Nor, generally, can the interpreter be constituted by the public body which has to administer the relevant law: for in that case the decision-makers would write their own laws. The interpreter must be impartial, independent both of the legislature and of the persons affected by the texts' application, and authoritative – accepted as the last word, subject only to any appeal. Only a court can fulfil the role.

38. If the meaning of statutory text is not controlled by such a judicial authority, it would at length be degraded to nothing more than a matter of opinion. Its scope and content would become muddied and unclear. Public bodies would not, by means of the judicial review jurisdiction, be kept within the confines of their powers prescribed by statute. The very effectiveness of statute law, Parliament's law, requires that none of these things happen. Accordingly, as it seems to me, the need for such an authoritative judicial source cannot be dispensed with by Parliament. This is not a denial of legislative sovereignty, but an affirmation of it: as is the old rule that Parliament cannot bind itself. The old rule means that successive Parliaments are always free to make what laws they choose; that is one condition of Parliament's sovereignty. The requirement of an authoritative judicial source for the interpretation of law means that Parliament's statutes are always effective; that is another.

III. The Common Law and Statutory Interpretation

The role of the common law courts as interpreters of Parliament's law is thus a central feature of the common law's place in the constitution. In chapter 1, I said that the exercise of statutory interpretation is very frequently value-laden, normative rather than descriptive, and cited the argument of Lord Mansfield – then William Murray, Solicitor General – in *Omychund v Barker*[4] in 1744: '[A] statute very seldom can take in all cases, therefore the common law, that works itself pure by rules drawn from the fountain of justice, is for this reason superior to an act of parliament.' Now I shall explain more fully the idea that the exercise of statutory interpretation is very frequently value-laden, normative.

We should regard this feature of statutory interpretation as entirely unsurprising. Consider these familiar truths to which I referred in chapter 1:

(a)   The common law has long held that criminal statutes must be interpreted strictly.
(b)   The same used to be true of taxing statutes, but that, perhaps, is less clear nowadays.
(c)   The courts lean against retrospective applications.

All of these are normative, not merely descriptive, positions; but they are part of the warp and weave of statutory construction, and regarded as elementary. They, and other nostrums of statutory interpretation, are the creatures, not of any rule

---

[4] *Omychund v Barker* (1744) 26 Eng Rep 14, 23.

laid down by Parliament, but of successive judges' perception of what may be derived from the foundational principles of the constitution. The rigour applied to criminal statutes springs from the principle that the State must prove criminal guilt strictly, according to the letter. The rigour that used to be applied to taxing statutes sprang from the principle, as it was then perceived, that private property likewise deserved strict protection from the incursions of the State. If tax law now favours the Revenue more, it is because of a shift in the principle: the good citizen should be ready to pay his or her tax according to the spirit, as well as the letter, of the law: so taxing statutes may be interpreted more purposively so as to emasculate artificial avoidance schemes. The rule against retrospectivity springs from the principle that the citizen should know what law applies to what he or she does: this was anyway a feature of the thin theory of the Rule of Law discussed in chapter 1. Between them these principles exemplify more general principles of the constitution: foundational principles – freedom, fairness, reason, legal certainty. These are in the keeping of the courts.

Many other examples may no doubt be found. My point is that in the act of construing statutes, the judges very often develop, refine and apply such constitutional principles; and in doing so, they make law. To the extent that the words of the Act do not dictate its interpretation – 'a statute very seldom can take in all cases' – it is necessarily so. Interpretation is supposedly the servant of Parliament's will. But it is an autonomous creative process. The old mantra that Parliament makes the law and the judges apply it was – is – a grave misunderstanding; and it obliterates the constitutional balance.

This autonomous creative process does not arise merely from the circumstance that 'a statute very seldom can take in all cases'. It is not just a matter of filling in gaps the legislature would itself have filled if the legislators had thought about it. The translation of words on a page into what should be done or not done is *of its nature* an autonomous creative process. Words on a page only come to life when they are interpreted; and more often than not there is more than one possible interpretation. Not because there are gaps; but because that is in the nature of language, especially a language as rich as English. Consider this utterance by a sometime *guru* of linguistics, Professor Noam Chomsky:

> Language is a process of free creation; its laws and principles are fixed, but the manner in which the principles of generation are used is free and infinitely varied. Even the interpretation and use of words involves a process of free creation.[5]

Or this from TS Eliot's 'Burnt Norton':

> Words strain,
>
> Crack and sometimes break, under the burden,
>
> Under the tension, slip, slide, perish,

---

[5] N Chomsky, Essay presented at a lecture at the University Freedom and the Human Sciences Symposium, Loyola University, Chicago, 8–9 January 1970.

Decay with imprecision, will not stay in place,

Will not stay still.[6]

Consider also this arresting passage in Plato's dialogue *Phaedrus*, in which Socrates, who never wrote down any of his philosophy, is discussing the written word:

Writing, Phaedrus, has this strange quality, and is very like painting; for the creatures of painting stand like living beings, but if one asks them a question, they preserve a solemn silence. And so it is with written words; you might think they spoke as if they had intelligence, but if you question them, wishing to know about their sayings, they always say only one and the same thing. And every word, when it is written, is bandied about, alike among those who understand and those who have no interest in it, and it knows not to whom to speak or not to speak; when ill-treated or unjustly reviled it always needs its father to help it; for it has no power to protect or help itself.[7]

Time and again there will be a choice how a text is to be interpreted – how it is to be given life: how its words are to have effect in the world. And time and again the choice will not be concluded by the language of the text. When it comes to Acts of Parliament the choice will be concluded (nearly always) within the constraints of the text, but very often also by the interpreter's view of what it should be taken to mean in light of basic principles of the common law: in light of the constitution's foundational principles. The very purpose of Acts of Parliament is to regulate what is and is not required, forbidden or allowed to the citizen or to the State, and this is the stuff of constitutional principle. The judicial act of statutory construction – the interpretive choice – makes law, because it insists that the statute complies with constitutional principle. The genius of the common law rests in the fact that it is ideally suited to the evolution of such principles. I shall come shortly to its methods.

Now let me turn to some concrete instances in which the courts make law in the act of construing statutes: instances in which it is not plausible to suggest that the act of interpretation does no more than give effect to the will of the legislature. Note these following examples.

First, the celebrated decision of the House of Lords in *Anisminic v Foreign Compensation Commission*.[8] The Commission made a determination that it had no power to make. But section 4(4) of the Foreign Compensation Act 1950 provided:

The determination by the commission of any application made to them under this Act shall not be called in question in any court of law.

And so the question arose: was it open to the court to correct the Commission's error? It was submitted that 'determination' meant a real determination and did

---

[6] TS Eliot, 'Burnt Norton' (1936), No 1 of *Four Quartets*.

[7] Plato, *Euthyphro. Apology. Crito. Phaedo. Phaedrus*, tr HN Fowler, Loeb Classical Library 36 (Harvard University Press, 1914) 275d–e.

[8] *Anisminic v Foreign Compensation Commission* [1969] 2 AC 147.

not include an apparent or purported determination that in the eyes of the law has no existence because it is a nullity. Here is a very familiar passage from Lord Reid's speech:

> Statutory provisions which seek to limit the ordinary jurisdiction of the court have a long history. No case has been cited in which any other form of words limiting the jurisdiction of the court has been held to protect a nullity. If the draftsman or Parliament had intended to introduce a new kind of ouster clause so as to prevent any inquiry even as to whether the document relied on was a forgery, I would have expected to find something much more specific than the bald statement that a determination shall not be called in question in any court of law. Undoubtedly such a provision protects every determination which is not a nullity. But I do not think that it is necessary or even reasonable to construe the word 'determination' as including everything which purports to be a determination but which is in fact no determination at all. And there are no degrees of nullity. There are a number of reasons why the law will hold a purported decision to be a nullity. I do not see how it could be said that such a provision protects some kinds of nullity but not others: if that were intended it would be easy to say so ...[9]

And so section 4(4) of the 1950 Act was construed to ensure that it did not prevent the court's supervision of subordinate bodies so as to confine their acts and decisions within the proper limits of the power given to them. Most certainly this was making law through the medium of statutory interpretation. But it was done to protect the Rule of Law, which of course underpins all our constitutional fundamentals.

The second case is *Witham*,[10] decided by the Divisional Court in 1997. Section 130(1) of the Supreme Court Act 1981 (now the Senior Courts Act) provided:

> The Lord Chancellor may by order under this section prescribe the fees to be taken in the Supreme Court ...

The Lord Chancellor made a statutory instrument, purportedly under the authority of section 130(1), increasing certain court fees payable on the issue of civil proceedings and revoking earlier provisions that relieved litigants in person who were in receipt of income support from the obligation to pay fees. The changes made it impossible for the applicant, who had no resources and relied on income support, to bring libel proceedings as a litigant in person. There was also evidence of other persons on very low incomes who were prevented from taking proceedings. In my judgment (with which Rose LJ agreed) I said:

> In my judgment the 1996 Order's effect is to bar absolutely many persons from seeking justice from the courts. Mr Richards' elegant and economical argument contains an unspoken premise. It is that the common law affords no special status whatever to the citizen's right of access to justice. He says that the statute's words are unambiguous,

---

[9] ibid 170–71.
[10] *R v Lord Chancellor, ex parte Witham* [1998] QB 575, 586F-G.

are amply wide enough to allow what has been done, and that there is no available *Wednesbury* complaint. That submission would be good in a context which does not touch fundamental constitutional rights. But I do not think that it can run here. Access to the courts is a constitutional right; it can only be denied by the government if it persuades Parliament to pass legislation which specifically – in effect by express provision – permits the executive to turn people away from the court door. That has not been done in this case.

The third case is *Cooper v Wandsworth Board of Works*, decided in 1863.[11] Statute forbade the erection of a building in London without giving seven days' notice to the local board of works, on pain of having the building demolished. A builder nevertheless began to erect a house in Wandsworth without having given due notice. The board of works sent men late in the evening to demolish it, thus doing exactly what the Act said they might do in the precise circumstances in which the Act said they might do it.[12] But the builder's action for damages for injury to the building succeeded. The court held that the board had no power to act without first asking him what he had to say for himself. In a well-known passage Byles J said this:

> [A] long course of decisions beginning with Dr Bentley's case, and ending with some very recent cases, establish that, although there are no positive words in a statute, requiring that the party shall be heard, yet the justice of the common law will supply the omission of the legislature.[13]

Reminiscent, perhaps, of William Murray in 1744, quoted near the beginning of this section: 'the common law, that works itself pure by rules drawn from the fountain of justice, is for this reason superior to an act of parliament'.

Lastly, *R v Registrar General, ex parte Smith*.[14] In that case the court had to consider section 51(1) of the Adoption Act 1976, by which the Registrar General owed a duty to disclose to the applicant, as an adopted person, his birth certificate. But the applicant had killed two people, one of whom he had thought was his foster mother; and if he obtained the certificate he was very likely to use the information to find and kill his birth mother. The court upheld the Registrar's refusal to disclose the certificate, reasoning that the statute was subject to an implied exception based on public policy, namely that statutory rights were not given to facilitate the commission of serious crimes.

These four cases are of course my selection; many others might readily be chosen. What should we make of them? As for *Anisminic*, I very much doubt whether anyone believes that Parliament actually intended that unlawful decisions of the Foreign Compensation Commission should be subject to what we now call judicial review for all the world as if section 4(4) of the 1950 Act did not

---

[11] *Cooper v Wandsworth Board of Works* (1863) 14 CB (NS) 180.
[12] HWR Wade and CF Forsyth, *Administrative Law*, 9th edn (Oxford University Press, 2004) 480.
[13] *Cooper* (n 11) 194.
[14] *R v Registrar General, ex parte Smith* [1991] 2 QB 393.

exist. As for *Witham*, I am quite certain that there was no actual legislative intention that section 130(1) of the Supreme Court Act 1981 would not authorise the changes in court fees which the Lord Chancellor purported to make; I apprehend that the intention of the legislators, or those who thought about it, was that the Lord Chancellor should have a free hand (subject to broad limits of reasonableness) in deciding what the court fees should be. *Cooper v Wandsworth Board of Works* (cited with approval in 1964 by Lord Reid in the landmark case of *Ridge v Baldwin*[15]) was, I suppose, not really a case of statutory interpretation at all. Certainly the result in *Cooper's* case plainly involved no inferences drawn from the statute, no implications derived from the text. It is a case where 'the common law [supplied] the omission of the legislature': a case, in other words, where the court held that the statute was deficient when it came to the protection of basic fairness in the shape of the right to be heard. As for *R v Registrar General, ex parte Smith*, no doubt Parliament would have excluded a right of access to the birth certificate of someone as dangerous as the applicant had the legislators thought about it; but presumably they did not.

In every one of these authorities the courts were concerned with the protection of constitutional fundamentals, and in none of them were the courts in truth giving effect to a legislative intention. I said in the Introduction that in chapter 8 I shall turn to the constitutional basis of judicial review, and at that stage I shall have more to say about the relation between the role of the courts and the notion of legislative intent.

IV. The Constitutional Balance

This brings me directly to the constitutional balance. The meeting of Parliament and the common law, in the crucible of statutory interpretation, is close to the core of it. Parliament's black-letter law puts the policy of democratic government onto the statute book. The courts' refinement and application of principle mediates the policy to the people. It provides as close a fit as possible between the policy of Parliament and those values – reason, fairness and the presumption of liberty – that over time have come to reflect and moderate the temper of the people.

A balance is therefore struck. The process is enriched by the fact that there are differences in kind between decision-making by the courts and decision-making by the legislature. I said in the last chapter that the common law is gradual, evolutive; but legislation is immediate. Parliament's law is not an evolutive or gradual process at all. Parliament can only make black-letter law. Though sometimes there are paving Acts that prepare the way for more to come; there may be provisions allowing Secretaries of State to go on and make detailed regulations; there may be long delays before the Act comes into force; and there may be – there very

---

[15] *Ridge v Baldwin* [1964] AC 40.

often are – amendments and re-amendments; still, generally, a statute is complete when it is passed, like the goddess Athena born from the head of Zeus. And it may be extinguished as completely, by another statute. Parliament's very sovereignty dooms its products to a transient, at least a precarious, existence. Whereas the courts hone and refine principles over time, the legislature creates new regimes at every turn. It may, and often does, reinvent the wheel. The courts do not. Courts and Parliament both make new lamps; but the courts make new lamps from old.

The life of our fundamental principles – reason, fairness and the presumption of liberty – lies in their application, case by case, over time. Their reality is of necessity evolutionary; much of their value consists in their capacity to adapt to changing times and conditions, while retaining a fundamental core. I shall work through this, as it applies in practice, in chapter 5, and shall address the refinements of substantive judicial review: the essence of the presumption of liberty; reason – from the *Wednesbury*[16] principle to the doctrine of proportionality; and fairness – from the Latin tags of natural justice to the principles of legitimate expectation.

Given their evolutive nature, these principles cannot be given life by the enactment of black-letter law. Parliament could no doubt enact a statute providing that public decisions shall be fair, reasonable and respect the presumption of liberty; but such a provision would be no more than words until the courts got to grips with it.

Next I shall describe the methods of the common law, in order to show how rich its contribution is to the constitutional balance, and how rich, therefore, is the ideal of the Rule of Law as it is found in this jurisdiction.

V. The Methods of the Common Law

The methods of the common law are fourfold: precedent, experiment, history and distillation. These elements operate together, in constellation with one another. Generally they involve what may be described as reasoning from the bottom up, not the top down. As a generality, we all know that the common law proceeds by the use of precedent, and it is with precedent – the rule of *stare decisis* – that I shall start.

A. Precedent

Ever since the Practice Statement of 1966,[17] the House of Lords, and now the Supreme Court,[18] has *not* been bound by its own previous decisions. Even so the

---

[16] *Associated Provincial Picture Houses Ltd v Wednesbury Corporation* [1948] 1 KB 223.
[17] Practice Statement [1966] 1 WLR 1234.
[18] *Austin v LB of Southwark* [2010] UKSC 78 [24] and [25].

Practice Statement says that their Lordships will '[treat] former decisions of this House as normally binding'. That, however, is a loose expression: it states no clear rule. What is meant is that the House will normally follow such decisions. That is not a rule of precedent at all but a rule of practice; and indeed, in practice the House departed from previous decisions only rarely and cautiously.[19]

The Court of Appeal, which is *de facto* the last court for the determination of most points of law in England and Wales, is bound not only by decisions of the Supreme Court but also by previous decisions of its own, save in a limited number of circumstances.[20] By contrast the High Court, though bound by the Supreme Court and the Court of Appeal, does not bind itself.[21] Now I do not suppose that the rules of precedent were evolved or designed to work as an integrated whole; but in looking for the methods of the common law, the combined effect of these precepts is worth considering as a single structure, a coherent system of *stare decisis*. If the High Court bound itself, the law would either ossify or there would be excessive calls on the Court of Appeal. If the Supreme Court bound itself, unjust and outdated law would persist – as was occasionally found before the Practice Statement – subject only to the possibility of legislative change. But if the Court of Appeal did *not* bind itself, the sacrifice of certainty would be unacceptably high. As it is, a balance is struck. It exemplifies the general balance the common law strikes between certainty and adaptability. This general balance is a child of the common law's methods, and it represents a large part of its genius.

And so this balance, struck by these different rules of precedent, constitutes a signal part of the contribution that is made by *stare decisis* to the methods of the common law; but this is not the only virtue of precedent. It produces a yet more subtle effect. It is that every principle has a tried and tested pedigree. It is refined out of what has gone before, and never constructed from untried materials.

But even the part it plays in honing our law over time is not the limit of precedent's subtlety. Consider how *stare decisis* works case by case. First you have to find the *ratio decidendi* of the previous judgment: the statement of law that decided the case. A statement of law that was not necessary for the earlier decision is not *ratio* and therefore not binding; a statement of law that is *ratio* but which can be said not to apply to the case in hand is not binding either – at least, not for the purpose of the present case, which will accordingly be distinguished on its facts from the earlier authority. These rules look quite rigid. A stranger visiting the common law from the universe of the civilians, where there is no principle of *stare decisis*, might be forgiven for thinking that their application is an almost mechanical process. It is nothing of the sort. Some precedents plant their seed, as it were, much more fruitfully than others; and it is certain that the ascertainment

---

[19] See, for example, *Knuller v DPP* [1973] AC 435.

[20] The leading case on *stare decisis* in the Court of Appeal is *Young v Bristol Aeroplane* [1944] KB 718.

[21] See also (in relation to the Divisional Court) *R v Greater Manchester Coroner, ex parte Tal* [1985] QB 67.

of a principle's scope, the reach of its precedent effect, is not a value-free exercise. It has a dynamic of its own.[22]

Some precedents, of course, flourish like the green bay tree: consider the *Wednesbury* case, about the reach of statutory public power: 'discretion must be exercised reasonably'.[23] The context was a local authority decision to close a cinema in a Midlands town on Sundays. I shall return to it in the next chapter. Lord Greene MR, Somervell LJ and Singleton J reserved their decision over a November weekend in 1947. It did not, I think, attract enormous attention at the time. Its significance as a major text in what we now call public law was not at first appreciated; perhaps because (if you agree with Lord Devlin, writing in 1956[24]) the English courts had lost the power to control the Executive. But the courts recovered the power to control the Executive; *Wednesbury* was rediscovered and became the leading authority on the reach of the judges' power of judicial review.

So there are precedents that prosper and there are precedents that falter and fail. The principles that survive, through generations of precedents, are the laws best fitted for their environment. It is a kind of Darwinian evolution. And because legal principles may be described (however roughly) as norms or rules, the survival of the fittest is a kind of *moral* success. The environment in which they must survive is an unruly one. It is the order of relations between one person and another and between citizen and State. Over time, if freedom, reason and fairness are cornerstones of the State's political philosophy, the effect of *stare decisis* is to hone and refine the law to reflect these cornerstones, to give them concrete form, and to make them more and more robust in their unruly environment. This is a moral process; that is to say, it is a process that enhances conscientious dealings between one person and another and between citizen and State.

B. Experiment

This aspect of the common law's method – experiment – is closely related to the first, precedent. I said earlier that it is a function of precedent that every principle acquires a tried and tested pedigree. It is refined out of what has gone before, and never constructed from untried materials. This is how the law of precedent actually works. In the first of his lectures on *The Nature of the Judicial Process*,[25]

---

[22] Note Lord Hope's comments in *Lagden v O'Connor* [2003] UKHL 64 [52], on the rule that the damages for which a defendant is liable cannot be increased by reason of the claimant's impecuniosity.

[23] *Wednesbury* (n 16) 229, per Lord Greene.

[24] Devlin LJ, 'The Common Law, Public Policy and the Executive', lecture to the Bentham Club, 28 February 1956, [1956] *CLP* 1.

[25] B Cardozo, *The Nature of the Judicial Process* (Yale University Press, 1921).

Benjamin Cardozo quotes this description given by an earlier American writer, Munroe Smith,[26] in 1909:

> In their effort to give to the social sense of justice articulate expression in rules and in principles, the method of the lawfinding experts has always been experimental. The rules and principles of case law have never been treated as final truths, but as working hypotheses, continually retested in those great laboratories of the law, the courts of justice. Every new case is an experiment; and if the accepted rule which seems applicable yields a result which is felt to be unjust, the rule is reconsidered. It may not be modified at once, for the attempt to do absolute justice in every single case would make the development and maintenance of general rules impossible; but if a rule continues to work injustice, it will eventually be reformulated. The principles themselves are continually retested; for if the rules derived from a principle do not work well, the principle itself must ultimately be re-examined.[27]

It is not I think fanciful to suggest that Munroe Smith's formulation recalls the approach of another philosopher (a very distinguished one), a generation or so later, to quite a different problem: the nature of scientific discovery. Professor Sir Karl Popper developed a theory of scientific discovery the towering importance of which has been consistently recognised since its first publication in 1934.[28] It is that science proceeds by postulating hypotheses that are only good so long as they are not disproved. Popper held that as a matter of logic, no number of positive outcomes at the level of experimental testing can confirm a scientific theory, but a single counterexample is logically decisive: it shows the theory, from which the implication is derived, to be false. The rigour of scientific method consists in its hypotheses being tested for falsity.

If the point is not pressed too far, Popper's falsification theory offers something of an analogy, not with the whole of the common law's method, but with Munroe Smith's description of its tentative, experimental aspect: just as Darwinian evolution offers something of an analogy with the doctrine of precedent. Both illuminate to some extent the workings of the common law.

The use and importance of experiment is illustrated by the *GCHQ* case,[29] decided in 1984; and the case will lead us towards the common law's two remaining methods, history and distillation. I shall look at this authority in a little detail. The Minister for the Civil Service, without prior consultation, issued an instruction forbidding staff at the Government Communications Headquarters from belonging to national trade unions. The case deals with two major creations of the common law: the royal prerogative power, and the judicial review jurisdiction. First, the prerogative. A question in *GCHQ* was whether exercise of the Crown's

---

[26] Munroe Smith (d 1926) was a distinguished legal academic at Columbia University. He was managing editor of *Political Science Quarterly* for many years.

[27] Cardozo (n 25) 23, quoting Munroe Smith, *Jurisprudence* (Columbia University Press, 1909) 21.

[28] K Popper, *Logik der Forschung* (Verlag von Julius Springer, 1935); English edn, *The Logic of Scientific Discovery* (Hutchinson, 1959).

[29] *CCSU v Minister for the Civil Service* [1985] AC 374 ('*GCHQ*').

prerogative power was subject to review in the courts. It was contended for the Minister, as Lord Fraser of Tullybelton summarised it,[30] that 'prerogative powers are discretionary, that is to say they may be exercised at the discretion of the sovereign (acting on advice in accordance with modern constitutional practice) and the way in which they are exercised is not open to review by the courts'. Here, then, was a question whether, in context, our public law imposed compulsory standards on public officials *at all*. But the case did not involve the exercise of the prerogative directly. The Minister's instruction had been given under the Civil Service Order in Council 1982. The Order in Council, but not the instruction, was a direct exercise of prerogative power. So there was a second issue: the Minister submitted that 'an instruction given in the exercise of a delegated power conferred by the sovereign under the prerogative enjoys the same immunity from review as if it were itself a direct exercise of prerogative power'.[31] Lord Fraser observed[32] that the first proposition advanced by the Minister was 'vouched by an impressive array of authority', which he proceeded to summarise. He went on to state that he 'would assume, without deciding, ... that all powers exercised directly under the prerogative are immune from challenge in the courts'.[33] As for the *indirect* exercise of the prerogative, Lord Fraser concluded, in agreement with Glidewell J at first instance,

> that there is no reason for treating the exercise of a power under article 4 [of the instruction] any differently from the exercise of a statutory power merely because article 4 itself is found in an order issued under the prerogative.[34]

Lord Brightman, like Lord Fraser, left review of the direct exercise of prerogative power to be considered in a case in which the issue had to be decided. But their other Lordships waded a little closer to the deep end. Lord Diplock said:

> My Lords, I see no reason why simply because a decision-making power is derived from a common law and not a statutory source, it should for that reason only be immune from judicial review.[35]

These *dicta* show the law moving forward on what may reasonably be called an experimental basis. Lord Scarman was more explicit, and wove precedent with experiment:

> Without usurping the role of legal historian, for which I claim no special qualification, I would observe that the royal prerogative has always been regarded as part of the common law, and that Sir Edward Coke had no doubt that it was subject to the common law: Prohibitions del Roy (1608) 12 Co Rep 63 and the Proclamations Case (1611) 12 Co Rep 74 ... Just as ancient restrictions in the law relating to the prerogative writs and

---

[30] ibid 397H.
[31] ibid 397H–398A.
[32] ibid 398B.
[33] ibid 398F–H.
[34] ibid 400C.
[35] ibid 410C.

orders have not prevented the courts from extending the requirement of natural justice, namely the duty to act fairly, so that it is required of a purely administrative act [I shall return to that in the next chapter], so also has the modern law … extended the range of judicial review in respect of the exercise of prerogative power. Today, therefore, the controlling factor in determining whether the exercise of prerogative power is subject to judicial review is not its source but its subject matter.[36]

See also Lord Roskill's speech.[37]

C. History

The *GCHQ* case has quite a lot to teach about the methods of the common law. First, much attention and respect is manifestly given to past learning. I do not mean the compulsory force of past learning as a matter of precedent; *GCHQ* points to a broader truth. In citing Coke,[38] Blackstone,[39] Chitty[40] and Dicey,[41] as well as later authority, their Lordships pay an implicit tribute to our constitution's virtuous power of continuity. Now this is a powerful driver of the relative tranquility of the British State. And it is a power driven by more engines than one; but a principal engine is the common law itself. This directs us to the third element in the fourfold methodology of the common law: history. In this respect the law's wisdom is the wisdom of Edmund Burke's vision of society, to which I referred in chapter 2, as a contract between the living, the dead and those who are yet to be born.[42] A hypothesis stands the test of time until there is a good reason to depart from it: in science, a factual reason based on evidence and experiment; in law, a normative reason based on social and political goods. It is a postulate of each of these worlds that change has to be justified. That is the respect the common law pays to its own history.

The second, connected lesson we may learn from *GCHQ* about the methods of the common law reflects more directly the analogy I have drawn with Popper's theory. The growth of modern administrative law, like a new scientific result, required a change (at least, the beginnings of a change) in the old order. The courts must be astute, in Lord Roskill's words,[43] not to 'hamper the continual development of our administrative law by harking back to what Lord Atkin once called … the clanking of mediaeval chains of the ghosts of the past'.

The change that *GCHQ* confirms is that by our present law, the determinant in any instance of the question whether the judicial review jurisdiction applies is

---

[36] ibid 407B–G.

[37] ibid 417B–H.

[38] In the quotation from Lord Scarman's speech, set out in section V.B. (see n 36).

[39] W Blackstone, *Commentaries*, 15th edn (1809), vol I, 251, 252. See Lord Fraser in *GCHQ* (n 29) 398B and Lord Roskill ibid 416H.

[40] J Chitty, *A Treatise on the Law of the Prerogatives of the Crown* (Butterworth & Son, 1820) 6–7: Lord Fraser in *GCHQ* (n 29) 398B.

[41] AV Dicey, *Law of the Constitution*, 8th edn (Liberty Fund Inc, 1915) 421 (Lord Fraser in *GCHQ* (n 29) 398B–C), 10th edn (Macmillan, St Martin's Press, 1959) 424 (Lord Roskill in *GCHQ* (n 29) 416F).

[42] E Burke, *Reflections on the Revolution in France*, ed LG Mitchell (Oxford University Press, 1993).

[43] *GCHQ* (n 29) 417C.

not the source of the power under review but its subject matter: see in particular the extract from Lord Scarman's speech in section V.B. This insight reflects Munroe Smith's perception: case law as working hypothesis, continually retested in the laboratories of the law. It recalls our analogy with Popper's theory: it tests the existing hypothesis for falsity. It discloses the second element in our methodology: experiment.

D. Distillation

The *GCHQ* case was not, of course, the law's last word on the prerogative. It was revisited in 1993 in a well-known case in the Divisional Court about the prerogative of mercy: *R v Home Secretary, ex parte Bentley.*[44] The applicant's brother was hanged in January 1953 for the murder of a police officer. His co-defendant, Craig, had fired the fatal shot; but Craig was only 16 and so did not face the death penalty. The applicant had campaigned for a posthumous pardon for her brother, and sought a judicial review when that was refused by the Home Secretary of the day.

Miss Bentley's judicial review succeeded. Now, there is what might be called a benign slippage between *GCHQ* and *Bentley*, which exemplifies the common law's experimental method at work, and also uncovers the last element in our fourfold methodology: distillation. The judgment in the later case, *Bentley*, has nothing to say of the distinction, which exercised Lord Fraser in *GCHQ*, between a direct and indirect exercise of the prerogative. The report of the argument has nothing to say about it either. But we can see from what Watkins LJ said that the old hypothesis about the prerogative, laying emphasis on the source of the relevant power as a touchstone of jurisdiction, has even more clearly given way to the new: that it is the subject matter of the decision and not the legal source that determines jurisdiction. A new outcome – review of the prerogative: justified by a new principle – subject matter not source. Reasoning from the bottom up, not the top down. The law of the prerogative was further distilled: distillation is the fourth of the common law's methods.

Now let me turn back to *GCHQ* and its other major theme: Lord Diplock's review[45] of the three heads under which judicial review may be brought. As is well known, the three heads of judicial review were illegality, irrationality and procedural impropriety. This was not new law. Subject to the criticism I shall level in chapter 5 against Lord Diplock's distinct approach to 'irrationality', it was a distillation; it placed the now well-established *Wednesbury* rule in a clear framework; and the tripartite division gave shape, and therefore principle, to the growing *corpus* of administrative law. This process of distillation possesses virtues beyond clarity, certainly beyond mere tidiness. It involves modification and adjustment. It helps expose potential gaps in the law: by articulating the present reach of the

---

[44] *R v Home Secretary, ex parte Bentley* [1994] QB 349.
[45] *GCHQ* (n 29) 410C–411C.

law, it maps the way to where it may reach hereafter. After naming the three heads of judicial review in *GCHQ* Lord Diplock added a footnote:

> That is not to say that further development on a case by case basis may not in course of time add further grounds. I have in mind particularly the possible adoption in the future of the principle of 'proportionality' which is recognised in the administrative law of several of our fellow members of the European Economic Community ...[46]

This process of distillation can be seen as itself a part, at least a facilitator, of Munroe Smith's 'method of the lawfinding experts'. As I said at the beginning, the four methods of the common law operate together, in constellation with one another. In the public law field the process of distillation has been busily employed in the years since *GCHQ*, building on Lord Diplock's formulation. The twin tides of Luxembourg and Strasbourg have rather dislodged *Wednesbury* from its pride of place on the foreshore of the law. But though the tides started across the Channel, their flood is in the common law.

E. Conclusions

In all of this we can see the common law's methods at work. Let me draw them together. First, there is an affinity between our two analogies, and thus the first two methods of the four. The process of evolution that precedent represents – our first method – has a dynamic: its force as a legal rule is strong or weak according as the legal principle in question is strong or weak. The experimental process described by Munroe Smith and encapsulated by the comparison with Popper's theory – our second method – has the same dynamic. Indeed I think our legal incarnations of Darwin and Popper point in much the same direction: while Darwin takes the shape of a compulsory rule, Popper has the form of experimental reasoning. As for the dynamic, the strength or weakness of any principle is tempered by the force of history, the law's third method, its role as an engine of the constitution's virtuous power of continuity. The first three methods promote and enliven the workings of the fourth: the distillation of the law, yielding ordered principle, giving space and time for further development. Evolution, experiment, history, distillation: these, then, are the methods of the common law, each in constellation with the others.

These four methods allow the common law to be innovative and conservative at the same time. Evolution and experiment invest it with a self-correcting quality. Through the four methods it digests social change and adjusts the law in the light of what it finds. But it is never *dirigiste*; it produces no new tables of the law from on high; it has no unique inspiration; it is not a single grand edifice. It is, if you like, more London than Paris. And it is uniquely suited to the development, maintenance and adjustment of the constitutional balance as era succeeds era.

---

[46] ibid 410D–E.

5

Reason, Fairness and the Presumption of Liberty

The foundational principles of reason, fairness and the presumption of liberty are the principal means by which concrete form is given to the constitutional balance between the two moralities, between legal principle and governmental power. Because their edges are not sharp and their wisdom depends upon their reach from time to time, the methods of the common law are especially suited to creating the balance in practice. The presumption of liberty is in some ways a more complex idea than the others.

I shall address reason first. In the Introduction I described it – in the sense in which it takes its place as a constitutional fundamental – as reason in the making and application of the law.

I. Reason – *Wednesbury* and Proportionality

A. *Wednesbury*

> This case, in my opinion, does not really require reference to authority when once the simple and well known principles are understood on which alone a court can interfere with something prima facie within the powers of the executive authority ...

So said Lord Greene in the *Wednesbury* case,[1] reserved over a weekend by the Court of Appeal in November 1947. It's quite a throw-away line given the reams of learning devoted to *Wednesbury* after it was re-discovered in the 1960s. *Wednesbury* established one of the central objective standards or norms that the courts bring to the task of adjudicating upon the legality of decisions of public bodies, including, conspicuously, central government: the principle of (un)reasonableness. It established an essential limitation – a constitutional limitation – that binds the use of discretionary public power.

---

[1] *Associated Provincial Picture Houses Ltd v Wednesbury Corporation* [1948] 1 KB 223, 231.

As I said in chapter 4, the context was a local authority decision to close a cinema in a Midlands town on Sundays. The Court of Appeal unanimously upheld the decision of the first instance judge, Henn Collins J, to the effect that the ban was within the proper powers of the decision-maker. Lord Greene did in fact make some 'reference to authority'. Here is the central passage of his judgment, in which he describes what has become known as the *Wednesbury* principle:

> It is true the discretion must be exercised reasonably. Now what does that mean? Lawyers familiar with the phraseology commonly used in relation to the exercise of statutory discretions often use the word 'unreasonable' in a rather comprehensive sense. It has frequently been used and is frequently used as a general description of the things that must not be done. For instance, a person entrusted with a discretion must, so to speak, direct himself properly in law. He must call his own attention to the matters which he is bound to consider. He must exclude from his consideration matters which are irrelevant to what he has to consider. If he does not obey those rules, he may truly be said, and often is said, to be acting 'unreasonably'. Similarly, there may be something so absurd that no sensible person could ever dream that it lay within the powers of the authority. Warrington LJ in *Short v Poole Corporation* [1926] Ch 66, 90, 91 gave the example of the red-haired teacher, dismissed because she had red hair. That is unreasonable in one sense. In another sense it is taking into consideration extraneous matters. It is so unreasonable that it might almost be described as being done in bad faith; and, in fact, all these things run into one another.[2]

This is a statement, an application, of what we may call the rule of reason. In more recent years, of course, largely under the influence of the Court of Justice of the European Union at Luxembourg and the European Court of Human Rights at Strasbourg, another principle of substantive review has taken its place in our public law: that of proportionality, to which I shall come. I mention it now because of the contrast often drawn with *Wednesbury*. Proportionality is generally said to be a more intrusive form of review; and this, I think, is compounded by a perception that the *Wednesbury* rule is not only remote, but also monolithic.

We need to consider the extent to which *Wednesbury* in fact promotes or mandates a hands-off, remote and monolithic form of judicial review. If it did, it would not readily reflect a characteristic of the common law that makes it so powerful an engine of the constitutional balance: its flexibility. I think *Wednesbury's* supposed remoteness was compounded by Lord Diplock's description of the principle in *GCHQ*.[3] In the central passage in Lord Diplock's speech there is first a gratuitous substitution of the term 'irrationality' for 'unreasonableness', then this:

> It [irrationality] applies to a decision which is so outrageous in its defiance of logic or of accepted moral standards that no sensible person who had applied his mind to the question to be decided could have arrived at it.[4]

---

[2] ibid 229.
[3] *CCSU v Minister for the Civil Service* [1985] AC 374 ('GCHQ').
[4] ibid 410.

Lord Diplock seems to be saying that the *Wednesbury* standard will only be breached if the decision-maker has gone off his head. Lord Carnwath criticised this formulation in the Annual Lecture of the Constitutional and Administrative Law Bar Association in 2013:

> [I]t is hard to see how 'outrage' can ever be an appropriate or acceptable part of the judicial armoury. And why 'logic'? The hallmark of a sound administrative decision, surely, is not so much logic, as informed judgment …[5]

This is an unsatisfactory criticism. Lord Carnwath misunderstands Lord Diplock's use of the term 'outrageous'. Plainly there is no intended reference to the judge's outraged feelings. The reference is to a decision that is wholly insupportable in logic or on the evidence. As for logic, I do not think its force should be disparaged: of course the law will strike down a decision that involves a self-contradiction or a *non sequitur*, unless the logical mistake is immaterial to the essence of the decision. I have thought for a long time that Oliver Wendell Holmes' famous *dictum*, 'the life of the law has not been logic; it has been experience', is no more than a partial truth. Logic and experience live together in the law.

i. A Variable Standard of Review

That said, Lord Diplock's formulation of the *Wednesbury* rule needs to be criticised, and not only for his gratuitous substitution of 'irrational' for 'unreasonable'. Its real flaw is that Lord Diplock misrepresents the principle enunciated by Lord Greene. If what he said was no more than a refinement or development of what Lord Greene had stated, well and good. But that is not the position. Here is the mistake: Lord Diplock's formulation – a decision that is 'outrageous' – reduces the principle to what is no more than a residual part of it: in Lord Greene's words, 'something so absurd that no sensible person could ever dream that it lay within the powers of the authority'. But it is plain that that is by no means the whole of the *Wednesbury* rule. The duty to have regard only to relevant considerations, which is a critically important dimension of the rule, has nothing on the face of it to do with absurdity or outrage. Nor does the duty not to misunderstand the evidence. If they did, the standard that *Wednesbury* sets would indeed be monolithic and remote; and virtually useless as one of the means of giving effect to the constitutional balance or, therefore, a guarantor of the Rule of Law as I have described it in chapter 1.

In reality *Wednesbury* encompasses perfectly everyday cases, where the decision-maker has not gone mad but has failed to take proper account of the material before him or her; and what *counts* as taking proper account will vary from case to case. The range of the principle's potential subject matter is as great

---

[5] Available at https://www.supremecourt.uk/docs/speech-131112-lord-carnwath.pdf.

as the range of things that public bodies have to decide. But this very fact demonstrates that *Wednesbury* does not set a monolithic standard. In some cases the material, or the evidence, is of a kind that may very readily be considered and assessed by a court. In others that is much less so. These will be instances where the exercise of discretion under challenge arises in a field of special sensitivity, such as national security or broad government policy, especially macro-economic policy. In such cases the assessment of material before the decision-maker either requires specialist, expert judgement, or has so many possible variables that there may be many viable answers, and which one is chosen will perfectly reasonably depend on political positions. Inevitably, a judicial review in such a case based on the *Wednesbury* principle will be correspondingly less intrusive.

This is the constitutional balance at work. Here are some examples. In *Ex parte Nottinghamshire CC*[6] in 1985, Lord Scarman said this:

> But I cannot accept that it is constitutionally appropriate, save in very exceptional circumstances, for the courts to intervene on the ground of 'unreasonableness' to quash guidance framed by the Secretary of State and by necessary implication approved by the House of Commons, the guidance being concerned with the limits of public expenditure by local authorities and the incidence of the tax burden as between taxpayers and ratepayers. Unless and until a statute provides otherwise, or it is established that the Secretary of State has abused his power, these are matters of political judgment for him and for the House of Commons. They are not for the judges or your Lordships' House in its judicial capacity.
>
> For myself, I refuse in this case to examine the detail of the guidance or its consequences … Such an examination by a court would be justified only if a prima facie case were to be shown for holding that the Secretary of State had acted in bad faith, or for an improper motive, or that the consequences of his guidance were so absurd that he must have taken leave of his senses.[7]

That was what might be called a 'hands-off' case – one concerned with what I have called macro-economic policy. Contrast the Court of Appeal's acceptance of a submission made by David Pannick QC (now Lord Pannick) in an important case about gays in the armed forces, decided in November 1995: *Smith & Ors v Ministry of Defence*.[8] The submission was as follows:

> The court may not interfere with the exercise of an administrative discretion on substantive grounds save where the court is satisfied that the decision is unreasonable in the sense that it is beyond the range of responses open to a reasonable decision-maker. But in judging whether the decision-maker has exceeded this margin of appreciation the human rights context is important. The more substantial the interference with human rights, the more the court will require by way of justification before it is satisfied that the decision is reasonable in the sense outlined above.[9]

---

[6] *R v Secretary of State for the Environment, ex parte Nottinghamshire CC* [1986] AC 240.
[7] ibid 247D–G.
[8] *Smith & Ors v Ministry of Defence* [1996] QB 517.
[9] ibid 554E–F.

Lord Bingham MR considered that this was an 'accurate distillation' of principles set out in two slightly earlier decisions of the House of Lords: *Bugdaycay*[10] and *Brind*.[11] In *Bugdaycay*, Lord Bridge stated that 'when an administrative decision under challenge is said to be one which may put the applicant's life at risk, the basis of the decision must surely call for the most anxious scrutiny'.[12] In *Brind*, he said 'we are ... perfectly entitled to start from the premise that any restriction of the right to freedom of expression requires to be justified and that nothing less than an important competing public interest will be sufficient to justify it'.[13]

All of these cases – *Smith*, *Bugdaycay* and *Brind* – were decided before the Human Rights Act was passed in 1998, let alone before it came into effect in October 2000. But they show that our public law was moving towards a recognition of the special importance of fundamental rights: I would say a recognition that such rights possess a constitutional status. The point is if anything given emphasis by the contrasting, hands-off approach to be found in Lord Scarman's strictures about judicial review of macro-economic policy in the *Nottinghamshire* case.

There is a passage in the speech of Lord Cooke of Thorndon in a post-Human Rights Act case, *R (Daly) v Secretary of State for the Home Department*[14] in 2001, where I am inclined to think Lord Diplock's mistake about *Wednesbury* is repeated, yet in the same breath (oddly, perhaps) the variable standard of review is recognised. This is what he said:

> And I think that the day will come when it will be more widely recognised that [*Wednesbury*] was an unfortunately retrogressive decision in English administrative law, in so far as it suggested that there are degrees of unreasonableness and that only a very extreme degree can bring an administrative decision within the legitimate scope of judicial invalidation. [There is the repetition of Lord Diplock's mistake. But Lord Cooke continues:] The depth of judicial review and the deference due to administrative discretion vary with the subject matter. It may well be, however, that the law can never be satisfied in any administrative field merely by a finding that the decision under review is not capricious or absurd.[15]

Wednesbury, then, imports a norm or standard that is based on the rule of reason but which bites more or less sharply according to the subject matter in the case. The question whether a public decision is 'beyond the range of responses open to a reasonable decision-maker', as it was put in the *Smith* case, is entirely contextual. There are some contexts in which there will be only one reasonable response; others where there will be many. It is a virtue of the *Wednesbury* rule, as it has been developed, that it allows for a flexible approach to judicial review that accommodates this contextual variation. Later in this chapter (see section II) I shall seek

---

[10] *Bugdaycay v Secretary of State for the Home Department* [1987] AC 514.
[11] *R v Secretary of State for the Home Department, ex parte Brind* [1991] 1 AC 696.
[12] *Bugdaycay* (n 10) 531G.
[13] *Brind* (n 11) 749A.
[14] *R (Daly) v Secretary of State for the Home Department* [2001] 2 AC 532.
[15] ibid para 32.

to demonstrate a similar flexibility in the law's application of the imperative of fairness, through the developing doctrine of legitimate expectations.

I have a postscript to *Wednesbury*. At the Bar, I once had a judicial review case in which my opponent was John Platts-Mills QC. In the course of his argument he contrived to draw a wonderful analogy between the *Wednesbury* principle and the General Confession in the *Book of Common Prayer*: '[w]e have followed too much the devices and desires of our own hearts' – bad faith; '[w]e have offended against thy holy laws' – failure to direct [oneself] properly in law; '[w]e have left undone those things which we ought to have done; and we have done those things which we ought not to have done' – irrelevant considerations; '[w]e have erred and strayed from thy ways like lost sheep ... there is no health in us' – an absurd (or Diplockian outrageous) decision. Many sources enrich the law.

B. Proportionality

In the last chapter I cited Lord Diplock's comment in *GCHQ*:

> I have in mind particularly the possible adoption in the future of the principle of 'proportionality' which is recognised in the administrative law of several of our fellow members of the European Economic Community ...[16]

The doctrine of proportionality originated in Europe and, as I have said, became embedded in our law as an import from Luxembourg and Strasbourg. Its place in our domestic law other than the contexts of the EU and human rights is still developing. The details are beyond the scope of this work.

What differences of principle are there between *Wednesbury* and proportionality? Both are tests of the edge or limit of public power. Though at this stage I am concerned with the foundational principle of reason (or reasonableness), both also feed the presumption of liberty, as I shall show. A much repeated formulation of the proportionality test is that given by Lord Sumption in *Bank Mellat (No 2)*:[17]

> The requirements of rationality and proportionality, as applied to decisions engaging the human rights of applicants, inevitably overlap. The classic formulation of the test is to be found in the advice of the Privy Council, delivered by Lord Clyde, in *De Freitas v Permanent Secretary of Ministry of Agriculture, Fisheries, Lands and Housing* [1999] 1 AC 69 at 80. But this decision, although it was a milestone in the development of the law, is now more important for the way in which it has been adapted and applied in the subsequent case-law ... [Its] effect can be sufficiently summarised for present purposes by saying that the question depends on an exacting analysis of the factual case advanced in defence of the measure, in order to determine (i) whether its objective is sufficiently important to justify the limitation of a fundamental right; (ii) whether it is

---

[16] *GCHQ* (n 3) 410D–E.
[17] *Bank Mellat v HM Treasury (No 2)* [2014] 1 AC 700.

rationally connected to the objective; (iii) whether a less intrusive measure could have been used; and (iv) whether, having regard to these matters and to the severity of the consequences, a fair balance has been struck between the rights of the individual and the interests of the community. These four requirements are logically separate, but in practice they inevitably overlap because the same facts are likely to be relevant to more than one of them.[18]

In the case of *Miranda*[19] I criticised Lord Sumption's fourth requirement – 'whether … a fair balance has been struck between the rights of the individual and the interests of the community'. I said:

> It appears to require the court, in a case where the impugned measure passes muster on points (i)–(iii), to decide whether the measure, though it has a justified purpose and is no more intrusive than necessary, is nevertheless offensive because it fails to strike the right balance between private right and public interest; and the court is the judge of where the balance should lie. I think there is real difficulty in distinguishing this from a political question to be decided by the elected arm of government.[20]

I draw attention to this criticism because it serves to emphasise a familiar but seemingly intractable difficulty about the concept of proportionality, which is that it tends to drive the court to judge the *merits* of decisions by public bodies, notably elected government. Such a function is beyond the remit of the *Wednesbury* doctrine. More generally, it may be regarded as unconstitutional, because it tends to usurp the right and duty of public authorities to exercise the powers given to them by the sovereign Parliament. If that is right, it constitutes an illegitimate trespass from the arena of judicial power to that of political power – in the language of this book's theme, it tilts the constitutional balance too far against the force of democratic government.

It is indeed common currency to treat proportionality as a more intrusive test for judicial review than *Wednesbury*. In *Daly*, Lord Steyn said that 'the proportionality test may go further than the traditional grounds of review inasmuch as it may require attention to be directed to the relative weight accorded to interests and considerations'.[21] In *SS (Nigeria)*,[22] I said '[t]here is no doubt that proportionality imposes a more demanding standard of public decision-making than conventional *Wednesbury* review, whose essence is simply an appeal to the rule of reason'.[23]

But that, I think, was over-simplistic, or at least insufficiently qualified. As I have said, *Wednesbury* encompasses a variable standard of review according to the subject matter of the case. That very fact puts *Wednesbury* in tune with Sumption's propositions (i) – 'whether [the measure's] objective is sufficiently important to

---

[18] ibid para 20.
[19] *Miranda v Secretary of State for the Home Department* [2014] 1 WLR 3140.
[20] ibid para 40.
[21] *Daly* (n 14) 1635E.
[22] *SS (Nigeria) v Secretary of State for the Home Department* [2014] 1 WLR 998.
[23] ibid para 38.

justify the limitation of a fundamental right' – and (iii) – 'whether a less intrusive measure could have been used'. It also sits well with Sumption (iv) – 'whether ... a fair balance has been struck between the rights of the individual and the interests of the community' – if, that is, one accepts Lord Sumption's proposition: as I have suggested, if it adds anything, it really amounts to an invitation to the court to embark upon a political judgement. As for Sumption (ii) – 'whether [the impugned measure] is rationally connected to [its] objective' – that is pure *Wednesbury*: if there were no such rational connection, the measure would be unreasonable as Lord Greene meant the term.

Properly understood, *Wednesbury* and proportionality are not quite so far apart. But proportionality does provide an added value. Sumption (i) and (iii) say more than *Wednesbury*, notwithstanding the latter's scope for a variable standard of review. In the same case of *SS (Nigeria)* I said this:

> [T]he true innovation effected by proportionality is not, in my judgment, to be defined in terms of judicial intrusion or activism. Rather it consists in the introduction into judicial review and like forms of process of a principle which might be a child of the common law itself: it may be (and often has been) called the principle of minimal interference. It is that every intrusion by the State upon the freedom of the individual stands in need of justification. Accordingly, any interference which is greater than required for the State's proper purpose cannot be justified. This is at the core of proportionality; it articulates the discipline which proportionality imposes on decision-makers.[24]

We shall see that the principle of minimal interference is part and parcel of the presumption of liberty. It encompasses, I think, Lord Sumption's requirements (i) and (iii), and also the two stages of the court's approach to proportionality envisaged by Dyson LJ in *Samaroo*:

> In deciding what proportionality requires in any particular case, the issue will usually have to be considered in two distinct stages. At the first stage, the question is: can the objective of the measure be achieved by means which are less interfering of an individual's rights? ... At the second stage, it is assumed that the means employed to achieve the legitimate aim are necessary in the sense that they are the least intrusive of Convention rights that can be devised in order to achieve the aim. The question at this stage of the consideration is: does the measure have an excessive or disproportionate effect on the interests of affected persons?[25]

I should emphasise that while proportionality should rightly be seen as a development of *Wednesbury*, there are dangers in its application. As I have said, it is common currency to treat proportionality as a more intrusive test for judicial review than *Wednesbury*; and to an extent that is so. The danger lies in deploying proportionality so intrusively as to usurp the proper function of elected government and so distort the constitutional balance. The danger has, I think, been exacerbated by the way in which the court's statutory jurisdiction under the

---

[24] *SS (Nigeria)* (n 22) para 38.
[25] *Samaroo v Secretary of State for the Home Department* [2001] EWCA Civ 1139 [19].

Human Rights Act 1998 has sometimes been exercised. I shall return to human rights in chapter 9.

All that said, the doctrine of proportionality has enriched the common law. In the third Hamlyn Lecture I said:

> Our law has embraced these legal importations from foreign sources as its own. They have become part of the means of the common law's power of continuous self-correction. They go in the scales of the constitutional balance; they have refined it, and lent it nuance. In making them our own we have re-fashioned them, or some of them, to bear the colour and stamp of common law principle.[26]

II. Fairness – *Ridge v Baldwin*; Legitimate Expectation

Proportionality and the *Wednesbury* rule are and remain building blocks of the Rule of Law: paradigms of the norms and standards the courts bring to the law, and major engines of the constitutional balance. The same is plainly true of the imperative of fairness. Fairness of course has many faces. Here I am concerned with fair procedures in public decision-making, which is the principal manifestation of fairness in the judicial review jurisdiction.

There was a time when the requirement of fair procedure was known as 'natural justice' and was more or less limited to two propositions: *audi alteram partem* and *nemo iudex in causa sua* – the rules of natural justice, as they were known. The scope of any such requirement, moreover, was thought to be limited to decisions that could be categorised as judicial or quasi-judicial. But the inherent limitations of these ideas have been blown away: the latter – the limitation of compulsory procedural standards to judicial or quasi-judicial decisions – by the case of *Ridge v Baldwin*,[27] decided by the House of Lords in 1963, and the former – the two Latin tags – very largely by the emergence in the common law of a general duty to act fairly and by the doctrine of legitimate expectation. Legitimate expectation started life as a construct of German administrative law, where it was called *Vertrauenschutz*. Its first appearance in our law seems to have been in Lord Denning's judgment in *Schmidt v Secretary of State*[28] in December 1968 – four years before our accession to what was then called the Common Market, and thirty years before the passing of the Human Rights Act 1998.

I shall come to those developments, but first there is something to say about the ethic of fairness. The evolution of principles of fair procedure exemplifies *par excellence* the application of justice. It is a paradigm of justice: fair procedure

---

[26] Lord Justice Laws, 'Lecture III: The Common Law And Europe', Hamlyn Lectures 2013 (27 November 2013) para 7, available at https://www.judiciary.uk/wp-content/uploads/JCO/Documents/Speeches/laws-lj-speech-hamlyn-lecture-2013.pdf.

[27] *Ridge v Baldwin* [1964] AC 40.

[28] *Schmidt v Secretary of State for Home Affairs* [1968] 2 Ch 149.

constitutes an ordinary, mainstream use of the very term, justice. Justice gives concrete effect to the constitutional balance. It does so by force of its Kantian ethic, whose contrast with the utilitarian ethic of government I discussed in chapter 3. I drew attention to the fact that the walls between these two are porous. Sometimes one trespasses into the other's territory; sometimes there is a legitimate and necessary cross-over or cooperation between them. It is important to recognise that the working of our foundational principles reveals that the norms and standards the judges bring to the law are by no means unaffected by utilitarian considerations. Since the distinction between the two moralities – Kantian and utilitarian – is central to the constitutional balance, we should mark the extent to which that contrast is qualified in practice. It happens most vividly in the context of fair procedures and the imperative of open justice.

In chapter 3 I referred to the use of special advocates and closed hearings in cases involving sensitive information touching national security. I return to this area now only to emphasise that the maintenance of principles that are integral to the constitutional balance is often a very practical struggle. The practice of conducting proceedings in private has been controversial: not only in security cases where the issue is whether the impugned person should be removed or deported from the United Kingdom as a risk to national security, but also in relation to civil claims where relevant and perhaps decisive evidence is security sensitive. What is to be done? If the evidence is excluded, the court may – perhaps will – arrive at an unjust result. If it is admitted and the case is heard in public, lives may be lost. A private hearing – sometimes only partly in private – may be seen as the lesser of two evils. Most difficult moral questions involve a choice between two evils; which is why firmness of purpose is an important virtue.

Open justice has sometimes to take a buffeting. Compromises of the kind I have described can be the struggle's best resolution; though of course bad compromises can be made. Neither the Rule of Law nor the constitutional balance is designed for Eutopia; in Eutopia, I suppose, you might not need the Rule of Law at all. The Rule of Law has to live in the practical world, and the practical world has rough edges.

A. *Ridge v Baldwin*

Ridge v Baldwin concerned the appellant's dismissal by the Watch Committee (which was the police authority) from his post as Chief Constable of the County Borough of Brighton. He had been given no opportunity to put his side of the story. I said at the start that *Ridge v Baldwin* blew away the limitation of compulsory procedural standards to judicial or quasi-judicial decisions; but it is not so simple as that. As Lord Reid's judgment shows, *Ridge* is a good example of how, as I put it in the last chapter, the courts make new lamps from old.

Lord Reid cites a long line of authority showing that the duty to hear the other side – *audi alteram partem* – was not limited to judicial or quasi-judicial decisions;

but in his view the then recent case law had taken a step backwards. He refers to the judgment of Lord Hewart CJ in *R v Legislative Committee of the Church Assembly, ex parte Haynes-Smith*,[29] in which it was sought to prohibit the Assembly from proceeding further with the Prayer Book Measure 1927. Lord Hewart in turn had referred to the judgment of Atkin LJ in *R v Electricity Commissioners*.[30] Lord Atkin had said this:

> The operation of the writs [of prohibition and certiorari] has extended to control the proceedings of bodies which do not claim to be, and would not be recognised as, Courts of Justice. Wherever any body of persons having legal authority to determine questions affecting the rights of subjects, and having the duty to act judicially, act in excess of their legal authority, they are subject to the controlling jurisdiction of the King's Bench Division exercised in these writs.[31]

Here is what Lord Hewart said in *Haynes-Smith*:

> The question, therefore, ... is whether ... either ... the Church Assembly as a whole, or ... the Legislative Committee ... is a body of persons having legal authority to determine questions affecting the rights of subjects, and having the duty to act judicially. It is to be observed that in the last sentence which I have quoted from the judgment of Atkin LJ the word is not 'or' but 'and'. In order that a body may satisfy the required test it is not enough that it should have legal authority to determine questions affecting the rights of subjects; there must be superadded to that characteristic the further characteristic that the body has the duty to act judicially ... As these writs in the earlier days were issued only to bodies which ... could be called, and naturally would be called Courts, so also today these writs do not issue except to bodies which act or are under the duty to act in a judicial capacity.[32]

Lord Reid opined that

> [i]f Lord Hewart meant that it is never enough that a body simply has a duty to determine what the rights of an individual should be, but that there must always be something more to impose on it a duty to act judicially before it can be found to observe the principles of natural justice, then that appears to me impossible to reconcile with the earlier authorities.[33]

He cited a great deal of law to bear out that observation. He considered that Lord Atkin's statement in the *Electricity Commissioners* case had been misunderstood; his discussion of that authority is illuminating.

Lord Reid considered that '[t]he authority chiefly relied on by the Court of Appeal in holding that the watch committee were not bound to observe the principles of natural justice was *Nakkuda Ali v Jayaratne*',[34] which concerned an order

---

[29] *R v Legislative Committee of the Church Assembly, ex parte Haynes-Smith* [1928] 1 KB 411.
[30] *R v Electricity Commissioners* [1924] 1 KB 171.
[31] ibid 205.
[32] *Haynes-Smith* (n 29) 415.
[33] *Ridge v Baldwin* (n 27) 75.
[34] Lord Reid in *Ridge v Baldwin* (n 27) 77, citing *Nakkuda Ali v Jayaratne* [1951] AC 66.

made by the Controller of Textiles in Ceylon. The Privy Council held that the Controller was not

> acting judicially or quasi judicially when he acts under this regulation. If he is not under a duty so to act then it would not be according to law that his decision should be amenable to review and, if necessary, to avoidance by the procedure of certiorari.[35]

The Privy Council proceeded to cite Lord Atkin in *Electricity Commissioners* and Lord Hewart in *Haynes-Smith* – 'there must be superadded to that characteristic the further characteristic that the body has the duty to act judicially'.[36] They considered that this amounted to 'a general principle that is beyond dispute'.[37]

Lord Reid considered that there was no such general principle. The law had taken a wrong turning in *Haynes-Smith* and *Nakkuda Ali*. The Watch Committee had been obliged to give the Chief Constable an opportunity to be heard. Their other Lordships agreed, save for Lord Evershed, who would have dismissed the Chief Constable's appeal. Both Lord Reid and Lord Morris of Borth-y-Gest cited Byles J's famous dictum in *Cooper v Wandsworth Board of Works*,[38] which I set out in chapter 4:

> A long course of decisions, beginning with *Dr Bentley's* case, and ending with some very recent cases, establish that although there are no positive words in a statute requiring that the party shall be heard, yet the justice of the common law will supply the omission of the legislature.

As I have said, Lord Evershed dissented. Some of his reasoning sounds very strange to modern ears:

> To insist, as I venture to think, on the invocation of these principles [ie of natural justice] whenever anyone is discharged from some office seems to me to involve a danger of usurpation of power on the part of the Courts and under the pretext of having regard to the principles of natural justice to invoke what may often be in truth little more than sentiment; and upon occasions when the Courts, though having necessarily far less knowledge of all the relevant circumstances, may be inclined to think that, had the decision rested with them, they would have decided differently from the body in question.[39]

It seems astonishing that Lord Evershed would deny a right to be heard to someone about to be sacked because a court upholding the right might be thought guilty of undue interference. Fortunately, his view did not prevail.

The immediate significance of *Ridge v Baldwin* is that it scotched the heretical notion that the requirements of fair procedure were limited to decisions that could be categorised as judicial or quasi-judicial. For our purposes, the case – not

---

[35] *Nakkuda Ali v Jayaratne* (n 34) 77.
[36] ibid 78, cited in *Ridge v Baldwin* (n 27) 78.
[37] ibid.
[38] *Cooper v Wandsworth Board of Works* (1863) 14 CB (NS) 180, 194.
[39] *Ridge v Baldwin* (n 27) 96.

least the speech of Lord Reid – is important for two further reasons. First, it illustrates the methods of the common law in action: the methods I described in the last chapter: notably precedent and distillation. But second, it has lessons for the constitutional balance. Lord Evershed surely put the balance in the wrong place. He would have immunised an important public body, the Watch Committee, against the discipline of one of our constitutional fundamentals, fairness. Had his view prevailed, it would no doubt have been denied to other public bodies also: on the spurious ground that they were not obliged to 'act judicially'.

B. Legitimate Expectation

The doctrine of legitimate expectation has taken the law of fairness into wider territory. As I have said, its first appearance in our law seems to have been in Lord Denning's judgment in *Schmidt v Secretary of State* in December 1968. It was well established by 1984, when in the *GCHQ* case Lord Fraser described it thus:

> Legitimate, or reasonable, expectation may arise either from an express promise given on behalf of a public authority or from the existence of a regular practice which the claimant can reasonably expect to continue.[40]

For a long time there was a degree of uncertainty and debate as to whether there might be substantive, as opposed to purely procedural, legitimate expectations: that is, whether there were circumstances in which the doctrine might require a public authority (notably government) not merely to consult affected persons before going back on a promise or practice, but actually to preserve existing policy so as not to deprive affected persons of a promised advantage. The high water mark of what might be called the 'procedure only' school of thought was perhaps *Ex parte Hargreaves*[41] in 1997.

However this debate has been effectively resolved so as to acknowledge the possibility of a substantive legitimate expectation. A decisive case was *Ex parte Coughlan*[42] in 2001. In *Bhatt Murphy*[43] I gave what I described as 'a very broad summary of the place of legitimate expectations in public law':

> The power of public authorities to change policy is constrained by the legal duty to be fair (and other constraints which the law imposes). A change of policy which would otherwise be legally unexceptionable may be held unfair by reason of prior action, or inaction, by the authority. If it has distinctly promised to consult those affected or potentially affected, then ordinarily it must consult (the paradigm case of procedural expectation). If it has distinctly promised to preserve existing policy for a specific

---

[40] *GCHQ* (n 3) 401B–C.

[41] *R v Secretary of State for the Home Department and Governor of Her Majesty's Prison Risley, ex parte Hargreaves* [1997] 1 WLR 906.

[42] *R v North and East Devon Health Authority, ex parte Coughlan* [2001] QB 213.

[43] *R (on the application of Bhatt Murphy – a firm) v The Independent Assessor* [2008] EWCA Civ 755.

person or group who would be substantially affected by the change, then ordinarily it must keep its promise (substantive expectation). If, without any promise, it has established a policy distinctly and substantially affecting a specific person or group who in the circumstances was in reason entitled to rely on its continuance and did so, then ordinarily it must consult before effecting any change (the secondary case of procedural expectation). To do otherwise, in any of these instances, would be to act so unfairly as to perpetrate an abuse of power.[44]

In the next paragraph I referred to an earlier judgment of mine in *Nadarajah*[45] and went on to say:

> I would only draw from *Nadarajah* the idea that the underlying principle of good administration which requires public bodies to deal straightforwardly and consistently with the public, and by that token commends the doctrine of legitimate expectation, should be treated as a legal standard which, although not found in terms in the European Convention on Human Rights, takes its place alongside such rights as fair trial, and no punishment without law. Any departure from it must therefore be justified by reference among other things to the requirement of proportionality (see *Ex p Nadarajah*, paragraph 68).[46]

I would in particular emphasise the reference in the first of these citations to abuse of power. In the earlier case of *Ex parte Begbie*,[47] I said that 'abuse of power has become, or is fast becoming, the root concept which governs and conditions our general principles of public law'.[48] See also, for example, paragraph 71 of Lord Woolf's judgment in *Ex parte Coughlan*. Abuse of power may, no doubt, be regarded as a shorthand for the collection of values represented by the various grounds for judicial review. Though I prefer to articulate the force of judicial review as giving effect to the Rule of Law by reference to the core principles of reason, fairness and the presumption of liberty, this emphasis on abuse of power – and *Begbie* is by no means the only case where it is to be found – serves to demonstrate how far we have come since Lord Evershed was able to say what he said in *Ridge v Baldwin*. He thought that the spread of natural justice 'would involve a danger of usurpation of power on the part of the Courts'; but in later years, the abuse of power by governmental bodies has seemed a much more pressing concern. The speech of Lord Reid in *Ridge v Baldwin* exemplified the methods of the common law at work in the refinement of the constitutional balance; so also have the modern developments of the law relating to legitimate expectations.[49]

---

[44] ibid [50].

[45] *R (on the application of Nadarajah) v Secretary of State for the Home Department* [2005] EWCA Civ 1363.

[46] *Bhatt Murphy* (n 43) [51].

[47] *R v Secretary of State for Education and Employment, ex parte Begbie* [2000] 1 WLR 1115.

[48] ibid 1129F.

[49] In the more recent Privy Council case of *UNITED Policyholder Group v Attorney General for Trinidad and Tobago* [2016] UKPC 17, Lord Carnwath gives an overview of the modern cases on legitimate expectation. There is a useful comment on the case by Joanna Bell of St John's College Cambridge in 'The Privy Council and the Doctrine of Legitimate Expectations Meet Again' (2016) 75(3) *CLJ* 449.

C. Overriding Public Interest

The cases on fair process, including *Bhatt Murphy* and *Nadarajah* (see section II.B), contain many references to the possibility that a legitimate expectation may be denied by the existence of an overriding public interest of which the Government is the guardian. It may take the form of a statutory duty owed by the public decision-maker (that was the case in *Ex parte Begbie*), or some other consideration such as the dictates of national security. In the former case, where the bite of statutory duty is clear, the expectation is bound to give way: there is no constitutional dilemma; indeed the court is doing no more nor less than acknowledging the effect of a sovereign statute. But often the public interest asserted by the decision-maker in opposition to the legitimate expectation's fulfilment is not a matter of statutory obligation but the force of a discretionary policy of the government, which the governmental decision-maker (naturally enough) claims should prevail. Such a case (and of course there are others, beyond the context of legitimate expectations) is at the pivot of the constitutional balance.

III. The Presumption of Liberty

A. Two Propositions

Consider these two propositions:

(a) For individual citizens, everything that is not forbidden is allowed.
(b) But for public bodies, and notably government, everything that is not allowed is forbidden.

See what this means: if the first proposition is denied, citizens' freedoms are fatally and viciously curtailed. They cannot go about their daily business without fear of random and arbitrary interference. If the second proposition is denied, any public body that was released from its coils might act not out of the trust reposed by its constituents but for its own self-serving ends. If the body were central government, such a state of affairs would at once enslave the people. It is I think noteworthy that the first proposition is reflected in Article 2(3) of the Czech Charter of Fundamental Rights and Freedoms: 'Everybody may do what is not prohibited by law and nobody may be forced to do what the law does not command.'

By the first proposition, private individuals' actions require no justification before the courts unless it is shown that an individual has infringed a settled prohibitory rule. But in the case of the public authority, the second proposition dictates that every decision it takes must be authorised by the terms of a positive legal power conferred upon it, whose limits it must not transgress. Under these beneficent principles, individuals' consciences are their own; their power to commit themselves to a morality based on their communion with others is sovereign, as is their power to repudiate it. But the public authority's good conscience is not a matter of choice; such an authority's whole existence reposes in its duties. This antithesis is the touchstone of a free, but organised community. It is notable that in totalitarian regimes these positions are generally reversed: for the individual citizen, everything that is not allowed is forbidden (or liable to be forbidden); but for the State, everything that is not forbidden is allowed. The individual must justify what he or she does, and the authorities of the State are free of any such legal constraint because they command, and can change or ignore, the law itself. That is the touchstone of a closed community, where the people are slaves to arbitrary power.

The presumption of liberty, as a formula, looks like a reference only to the first of our two propositions. But in reality it embraces both. The security of the first – for the individual citizen, everything that is not forbidden is allowed – is critically dependent on the efficacy of the second – for government, everything that is not allowed is forbidden. If this latter principle is departed from, the presumption of liberty is at an end, for the power of the State would then be arbitrary, and tyranny is always – nearly always – the consequence of arbitrary power.

I referred to the contrast between these two propositions in a judicial review case called *Ex parte Fewings*[50] in 1995. It concerned the legality or otherwise of a ban imposed by a local authority upon stag hunting over part of its land:

> Public bodies and private persons are both subject to the Rule of Law; nothing could be more elementary. But the principles which govern their relationships with the law are wholly different. For private persons, the rule is that you may do anything you choose which the law does not prohibit. It means that the freedoms of the private citizen are not conditional upon some distinct and affirmative justification for which he must burrow in the law books. Such a notion would be anathema to our English legal traditions. But for public bodies, the rule is opposite, and so of another character altogether. It is that any action to be taken must be justified by positive law. A public body has no heritage of legal rights which it enjoys for its own sake; at every turn, all of its dealings constitute the fulfilment of duties which it owes to others; indeed, it exists for no other purpose. ... it has no rights of its own, no axe to grind beyond its public responsibility: a responsibility which defines its purpose and justifies its existence. Under our law, this is true of every public body. The rule is necessary in order to protect the people from arbitrary interference by those set in power over them.[51]

The reality is that our two propositions support a single constitutional principle the effect of which is that State power is confined by law so as to secure the liberty of the people. This is what I have called the 'presumption of liberty'. The presumption of liberty is a principal guarantor of the Rule of Law as I have sought to explain the term. Let me align the importance of the presumption of liberty with what I said about the Rule of Law in chapter 1.

---

[50] *R v Somerset County Council, ex p Fewings* [1995] 1 All ER 513. The case went to the Court of Appeal, but this passage was not I think disapproved.
[51] ibid 524.

B. The Presumption of Liberty and the Rule of Law

In chapter 1, I said that the Rule of Law implies the deployment of objective standards in the interpretation and development of the law. Applied to Acts of Parliament, such standards travel beyond the requirement that statute law should be interpreted according to the ordinary meaning of its text. As Lord Mansfield's argument in *Omychund*[52] shows, very often the language will not cover every case. No less often, the language may be capable of more than one interpretation. I have discussed this more fully in chapter 4. In all these cases the judges will apply standards that constitute norms for the regulation of the conduct of persons and bodies subject to the law in question. The core standards are reason, fairness and the presumption of liberty. The application of these standards means that the judge will always look for the edge, the limit, of the power the statute gives to the ruler, and will do so with no bias in the ruler's favour. If it were otherwise, the judge would merely be the ruler's cypher. Then there would be no Rule of Law. This marries with what I said in chapter 2 on democracy: the scope of the foundational principles is endlessly contentious; they mark the very points where democratic and judicial power are liable to disagree. The resolution of such disagreements define the edge of the power statute gives to government.

Our three foundational principles, then, drive the Rule of Law and condition the democracy. But something is missing from what I have so far said about the presumption of liberty.

C. The Principle of Minimal Interference

How does the law find the edge of power – how does it measure what may properly be forbidden to private individuals, or what may properly be allowed to public bodies? These look like two questions but are in fact one. Broadly at least, every accretion of power to the State constitutes a permission to curtail the freedom of individuals. Even a power to distribute bounty: for that depends on a power to collect tax. The judicial review jurisdiction looks for the edge of this curtailment of individual freedom by State power, and does so by translating our foundational principles into case law. But the two propositions I have so far stated as giving content to the presumption of liberty do not tell the courts where or how to measure what may properly be forbidden to private individuals, or what may properly be allowed to public bodies.

A step on the way towards finding the answer consists in a third proposition, which takes its place alongside the first two as integral to the presumption of liberty. It is that every intrusion by the State upon the freedom of the individual stands in

---

[52] *Omychund v Barker* (1744) 26 Eng Rep 14, 26 ER 15; see ch 1, section VI.

need of objective justification. Our first two propositions do not entail this further proposition. It must be separately fought for. I (and others) have described it as the principle of minimal interference. I referred to it in discussing proportionality earlier (see section I.B). I cited a judgment of mine in *SS (Nigeria)*, in which I said that 'every intrusion by the State upon the freedom of the individual stands in need of justification. Accordingly, any interference which is greater than required for the State's proper purpose cannot be justified. This is at the core of proportionality.' My point at this stage is to emphasise that it is also at the core of the presumption of liberty.

Our three propositions, which together constitute the presumption of liberty, are a necessary function of independent adjudication. Ultimately, alongside the principles of reason and fairness, they are the incarnation of the very idea of government under law. These foundational principles are the means by which the common law, through the judicial review jurisdiction, finds the edge of political or governmental power. The process is honed and refined by the fourfold method of the common law: precedent, experiment, history and distillation. These are the tools that translate the high level of generality of our foundational principles into effective case law, and that is what gives life to the Rule of Law. It is one arm, the judicial arm, in the scales of the constitutional balance.

IV. Postscript – Forerunners of Judicial Review

We shall have a clearer idea of judicial review's place in the Rule of Law if we consider some aspects of its evolution. There is a great deal to be learnt from Sir Stephen Sedley's collection of essays, *Lions under the Throne*,[53] and I should pay tribute to the use I have made of it in what follows.

It is characteristic of the common law's fourfold method that some of our leading modern public law cases – cases that have played their part in striking the balance between private right and public interest – have their forebears in the shape of analogous judicial decisions, some taken a very long time ago. It will be helpful to look briefly at these before coming to the modern cases themselves. They exemplify the characteristics of the common law I have already described: notably its power of evolution and its continuity.

Stephen Sedley notes predecessors to the *Wednesbury*[54] case, the *Padfield*[55] case and *Anisminic*.[56] The oldest is *Wednesbury*'s forerunner, *Rooke's Case*,[57]

---

[53] S Sedley, *Lions under the Throne: Essays on the History of English Public Law* (Cambridge University Press, 2015).
[54] *Wednesbury* (n 1).
[55] *Padfield v Minister of Agriculture, Fisheries and Food* [1968] AC 997.
[56] *Anisminic v Foreign Compensation Commission* [1969] 2 AC 147.
[57] *Rooke's Case* (1598) 5 Co Rep 99b.

decided in 1598. This was a challenge to a decision of the commissioners of sewers. They had levied the entire cost of repairing a river bank on the riparian owner, thus allowing his neighbours to benefit from the repair without contributing to its cost. The commissioners' response to the challenge was that the levy was a matter for their judgement, and not for the court. Here is Sir Edward Coke's riposte:

> [N]otwithstanding the words of the commission give authority to the commissioners to do according to their discretions, yet their proceedings ought to be limited, and bound with the rule of reason and law. For discretion is a science or understanding to discern between falsity and truth, between wrong and right, between shadows and substance, between equity and colourable glosses and pretences, and not to do according to their wills and private affections …[58]

The language is not of course the language of Lord Greene in the *Wednesbury* case, though the reference to 'the rule of reason' reflects it precisely. And in 1598 the judicial review jurisdiction was certainly not deployed to control the actions of government, then in the hands of the reigning sovereign. But the seeds of what we would call the *Wednesbury* principle are there, and the sense of what is just comes through the sixteenth-century prose.

The next case is *Padfield*'s predecessor. *Padfield* decided that discretionary action taken under statute, if it is to be lawful, has to promote the policy and objects of the enabling Act. In the *Case of Monopolies*,[59] decided or reported the year after *Rooke's Case*, a man called Darcy sued a haberdasher for infringing a monopoly granted to him by the Queen. Popham CJ held that all monopoly was contrary to law because it restricted employment. He observed also that although the preamble to Darcy's grant recited that the Queen's purpose in making it was to advance the public good, yet all it had done was fill Darcy's pocket; and so, said the Chief Justice, 'the Queen was deceived in her grant': that is, the monopoly had not served the purpose for which it was given – the idea which informs the *Padfield* case.

The last in this trio of predecessors is a forerunner of *Anisminic*: *R v Derbyshire JJ*[60] in 1759. Here is Stephen Sedley's summary:

> [T]he King's Bench granted certiorari to quash an ultra vires order of quarter sessions requiring outgoing highway surveyors to make over their funds to an incoming surveyor, despite the prohibition [in a statute of William and Mary] against granting certiorari to quash 'any order made by virtue of this Act', on the ground that this did not protect orders made without jurisdiction.[61]

We can see the same approach in that case, over 250 years ago, to a statutory provision ousting judicial review – a no certiorari clause – as we find in their Lordships'

---

[58] ibid 210.
[59] *Case of Monopolies* 11 Co Rep 84, (1599) 74 ER 1131.
[60] *R v Derbyshire JJ* (1759) 2 Keny 299.
[61] Sedley (n 53) 61, fn 36.

speeches in *Anisminic*. I should add that Professor David Feldman, in his essay 'Anisminic in Perspective', notes the cases cited by Browne J at first instance in *Anisminic* to support the proposition that

> [no certiorari clauses] had been increasingly common in legislation since the nineteenth century, and it had been well established for a century or more that they excluded the courts' jurisdiction if a decision was within the jurisdiction of an inferior body, but not if it was outside it.[62]

The common law is always different, and always the same.

---

[62] D Feldman, 'Anisminic Ltd v Foreign Compensation Commission [1968]: In Perspective' in S Juss and M Sunkin (eds), *Landmark Cases on Public Law* (Hart Publishing, 2017) ch 4, pp 66–67. The cases (referred to ibid fn 21) are: *Evans v McLoughlan* (1861) 4 LT 31, 33, 34, 35, HL; *R v Mahony* [1910] 2 IR 695, 738, 743, 750; *R v Nat Bell Liquors* [1922] 2 AC 128, PC, 152; *The State v O'Donnell* [1945] IR 126, 161; *R v Northumberland Compensation Appeal Tribunal, ex parte Shaw* [1952] 1 KB 338, CA, 716 *per* Lord Goddard CJ; *R v Medical Appeal Tribunal, ex parte Gilmore* [1957] 1 QB 574, 586, 588; *R v Hurst, ex parte Smith* [1960] 2 QB 133, DC.

6

Finding the Edge: Judicial Deference

In chapter 3, I said that judicial deference marks the space the law must give to the democratic power. It is one of the ways in which the courts articulate the limit or edge of the lawful power of government. Another is the creative use of statutory interpretation, as I described it principally in chapter 4: a value-laden, normative exercise, by which the judges frequently develop, refine and apply constitutional principle. These two judicial functions promote the constitutional balance. Judicial deference pulls in favour of democratic power and the utilitarian morality of government. Creative statutory interpretation pulls in favour of constitutional principle and the Kantian morality of the common law. These contrasting forces condition the courts' duty in any given case to find the edge or limit of statutory public power: the very means by which independent adjudication lifts the Rule of Law above the thin theory. Lord Sumption thinks[1] that judicial deference has gone too far. I disagree.

This chapter is more particularly concerned with judicial deference.

I. Introductory Cases

I shall start with some authority which conveniently introduces the notion of judicial deference. In *Kebilene*,[2] Lord Hope of Craighead said this:

> In this area [ie the law of human rights] difficult choices may have to be made by the executive or the legislature between the rights of the individual and the needs of society. In some circumstances it will be appropriate for the courts to recognise that there is an area of judgment within which the judiciary will defer, on democratic grounds, to the considered opinion of the elected body or person whose act or decision is said to be incompatible with the Convention. This point is well made at p 74, para 3.21 of *Human Rights Law and Practice*[3] ... where the area in which these choices may arise is conveniently and appropriately described as the 'discretionary area of judgment'. It will be easier for such an area of judgment to be recognised where the Convention itself requires a balance to be struck, much less so where the right is stated

---

[1] *The Reith Lectures* (2019).
[2] *R v DPP, ex parte Kebilene* [2000] 2 AC 326.
[3] Then the 1999 edition, now Lord Lester of Herne Hill, Lord Pannick and J Herberg (eds), *Human Rights Law and Practice*, 3rd edn (Butterworths, 2009).

in terms which are unqualified. It will be easier for it to be recognised where the issues involve questions of social or economic policy, much less so where the rights are of high constitutional importance or are of a kind where the courts are especially well placed to assess the need for protection.[4]

And in *Brown v Stott*,[5] Lord Bingham of Cornhill said this:

> Judicial recognition and assertion of the human rights defined in the Convention is not a substitute for the processes of democratic government but a complement to them. While a national court does not accord the margin of appreciation recognised by the European Court as a supra-national court, it will give weight to the decisions of a representative legislature and a democratic government within the discretionary area of judgment accorded to those bodies ...[6]

The application of this 'discretionary area of judgment' – judicial deference – is particularly to the fore where the subject of adjudication is one of the political rights enshrined in Articles 8–11 of the European Convention on Human Rights (to which I shall come in more detail in chapter 9), notably the right to respect for private and family life given by Article 8. But the need for judicial deference has to be considered whenever, as I said in chapter 3, the court is carrying out a proportionate adjudication between private right and public interest: whenever, that is to say, it has to decide the force to be accorded to the utilitarian morality of government. In a dissenting judgment in *International Transport Roth GmbH* I said:

> In the ... case where ... a balance has to be struck between contradictory interests each possessing some substance of legitimacy, a critical factor in the court's appreciation of the balance will be the degree or margin of deference it pays to the democratic decision-maker. This deference – and its limits – have to be fashioned in a principled but flexible manner, sensitive to the particular case and its context. In some contexts the deference is nearly absolute. In others it barely exists at all. The development of principle in this field is one of the most important challenges which the common law must meet, in face of the provisions of the HRA [Human Rights Act] and our own domestic acceptance of the idea of constitutional rights.[7]

And in *Brown v Stott*, Lord Steyn cited *Human Rights Law and Practice*:[8]

> Just as there are circumstances in which an international court will recognise that national institutions are better placed to assess the needs of society, and to make difficult choices between competing considerations, so national courts will accept that there are some circumstances in which the legislature and the executive are better placed to perform those functions.[9]

---

[4] *Kebilene* (n 2) 381B–C.
[5] *Brown v Stott (Procurator Fiscal, Dunfermline)* [2003] 1 AC 681.
[6] ibid 703C–D.
[7] *International Transport Roth GmbH v Secretary of State for the Home Department* [2003] QB 728, para 75.
[8] See n 3.
[9] *Brown v Stott* (n 5) 711B–C.

II. Lord Hoffmann in the *ProLife* Case

The authorities cited in section I (and there are of course others) give the flavour of judicial deference. I shall turn next to criticise some observations of Lord Hoffmann, who deprecated the language of deference in the case of *ProLife Alliance*[10] in these terms:

> 75. My Lords, although the word 'deference' is now very popular in describing the relationship between the judicial and the other branches of government, I do not think that its overtones of servility, or perhaps gracious concession, are appropriate to describe what is happening. In a society based upon the Rule of Law and the separation of powers, it is necessary to decide which branch of government has in any particular instance the decision-making power and what the legal limits of that power are. That is a question of law and must therefore be decided by the courts.
>
> 76. This means that the courts themselves often have to decide the limits of their own decision-making power. That is inevitable. But it does not mean that their allocation of decision-making power to the other branches of government is a matter of courtesy or deference. The principles upon which decision-making powers are allocated are principles of law. The courts are the independent branch of government and the legislature and executive are, directly and indirectly respectively, the elected branches of government. Independence makes the courts more suited to deciding some kinds of questions and being elected makes the legislature or executive more suited to deciding others. The allocation of these decision-making responsibilities is based upon recognised principles. The principle that the independence of the courts is necessary for a proper decision of disputed legal rights or claims of violation of human rights is a legal principle. It is reflected in article 6 of the Convention. On the other hand, the principle that majority approval is necessary for a proper decision on policy or allocation of resources is also a legal principle. Likewise, when a court decides that a decision is within the proper competence of the legislature or executive, it is not showing deference. It is deciding the law.

I think this passage mistakes the sense accorded to the term 'deference' in the cases about review of discretionary power, and if read literally would have some startling consequences. 'Deference', as the term is used in the cases, has nothing to do with servility or gracious concession. Rather, it marks the courts' recognition that the public body – often central government – to which discretionary power has been delegated by Parliament is the primary decision-maker as to how the power should be used; such a recognition is required if effect is to be given to Parliament's authority as the source of the power in question. The courts' role is generally secondary, though as we shall see in chapter 9, that is a problematic proposition when it comes to the law of human rights.

---

[10] *R (on the application of ProLife Alliance) v BBC* [2004] 1 AC 185, paras 75–76.

Some observations of Lord Bridge in the case of *Brind*,[11] which concerned the Government's prohibition of broadcasts of the direct speech of persons representing terrorist organisations, illustrate this dual role:

> The primary judgment as to whether the particular competing public interest justifies the particular restriction imposed falls to be made by the Secretary of State to whom Parliament has entrusted the discretion. But we are entitled to exercise a secondary judgment by asking whether a reasonable Secretary of State, on the material before him, could reasonably make that primary judgment.[12]

Lord Hoffmann in *ProLife* also, I think, gives the impression that the search for the edge, the limit, of the power in question can simply be deduced from existing principles, and in any given case the power of decision is either in the hands of the courts or in the hands of government. It is here that we find the startling consequences to which I referred earlier: the exclusive possession of State power by one or other arm of government. Certainly the place where the edge is to be found is a matter of law for the courts: but the search is nuanced, sometimes difficult, and greatly coloured by the circumstances of the particular case. This view is reflected, I think, in some observations of Professor Trevor Allan in *The Sovereignty of Law*:

> Insofar ... as Hoffmann suggests that different sorts of decision must be allocated exclusively to particular branches, regardless of the particular circumstances in which the issue of separation of powers arises, the dictum carries a threat to the Rule of Law. In practice, governmental decisions will typically engage both matters of principle, including the demands of individual rights, and matters of policy or allocation of resources, including the reasonable limits to particular rights that broader public interests legitimately require. Adherence to an inflexible doctrine of separation of powers would preclude the far-reaching judicial inquiry that the appropriate balance between private and public interests demands.[13]

Professor Allan's emphasis on the threat to the Rule of Law is surely right. Hoffmann indeed suggests that different sorts of decision must be allocated *exclusively* to particular branches – courts or government: 'it is necessary to decide which branch of government has in any particular instance the decision-making power'. Read literally, this would appear to mean that in those cases where government is the decision-maker, the courts would have no role. But that is a denial of the very process of judicial review, by which, of course, governmental decisions are supervised by the judges for their legality. Lord Hoffmann cannot have failed to understand that; so he must have meant something else. But what can it have been? I cannot find a sensible answer. If Lord Hoffmann would have subscribed to Lord Bridge's surely uncontentious formula in the *Brind* case – 'we are entitled

---

[11] *R v Secretary of State for the Home Department, ex parte Brind* [1991] 1 AC 696.
[12] ibid 749A–B.
[13] TRS Allan, *The Sovereignty of Law* (Oxford University Press, 2013) 29.

to exercise a secondary judgment by asking whether a reasonable Secretary of State … could reasonably make [the] primary judgment' – then the criticism of the language of deference as betraying 'overtones of servility' becomes incoherent: servility obviously has nothing to do with it.

More than this, Lord Hoffmann's simplistic allocation of areas of legal power exclusively to one or other branch of the State – courts or government – closes the door on the subtlety of the constitutional balance. At the core of the constitutional balance is the moderating effect of fundamental principles – reason, fairness and the presumption of liberty – on the force of democratic power. The two moralities jostle for position. Although, as I have shown, courts and government sometimes trespass into each other's domain without sufficient cause (the courts do so when, 'usually on the springboard of proportionality, [they] pay insufficient respect to the margin of discretion the government decision-maker enjoys'[14]), still it is inevitable that there should be some cross-over between them. The constitutional balance is achieved, or at least respected, when the morality of law is brought to bear on the morality of government; and that would be impossible if they were hermetically sealed one from the other.

III. Why Should the Courts Defer to Democratic Power?

On top of these criticisms, the passage from Lord Hoffmann's speech in *ProLife* gives no clue as to the basis upon which in some areas the courts should defer to government, beyond the terse statement that '[i]ndependence makes the courts more suited to deciding some kinds of questions and being elected makes the legislature or executive more suited to deciding others'. Now, I have said that judicial deference is one of the ways in which the courts articulate the limit or edge of governmental statutory power; but it will be of little help as such an instrument unless there is some principled or at least pragmatic ground on which deference is due. I have suggested that deference marks the courts' recognition that as regards the merits of the use of discretionary power in any given instance, the public body to which the power has been delegated by Parliament is the primary decision-maker; that is required if effect is to be given to Parliament's authority as the source of the power in question. This is an implicit claim that (to put it broadly at this stage) deference is due, at least to some extent and in some circumstances, to the elected arms of government precisely because they are elected: it is due, that is to say, to the democracy.

The *Wednesbury*[15] case might be said to exemplify the call for deference on democratic grounds. Time and again it has been stated that *Wednesbury* demonstrates an imperative that the judges should not trespass – at least not too far – into

---

[14] See ch 3, section II.C.
[15] *Associated Provincial Picture Houses Ltd v Wednesbury Corporation* [1948] 1 KB 223.

the merits of decisions by Parliament's delegates. It is true that in chapter 5 I was at pains to insist that *Wednesbury* imports a variable standard of review, and so it does; but it is certainly not a mechanism by which the courts routinely re-decide issues that have been assigned to Ministers or other public bodies. And even proportionality – commonly understood to be more intrusive than *Wednesbury* – is not to be deployed so as to usurp the proper function of elected government.

In *SS (Nigeria)*[16] I cited *Brown v Stott*,[17] *R v Lambert*,[18] *Poplar v Donoghue*,[19] *Marcic v Thames Water Utilities Ltd*[20] and *R v Lichniak*[21] to support the proposition that where the decision-maker is Parliament, the primary legislator, and not merely the executive, the discretionary area of judgement accorded to it by the courts will be especially wide; and in *International Transport Roth GmbH* I said this:

> 83. [T]he first principle which I think emerges from the authorities is that greater deference is to be paid to an Act of Parliament than to a decision of the executive or subordinate measure ... Where the decision-maker is not Parliament, but a minister or other public or governmental authority exercising power conferred by Parliament, a degree of deference will be due on democratic grounds – the decision-maker is Parliament's delegate – within the principles accorded by the cases. But where the decision-maker is Parliament itself, speaking through main legislation, the tension of which I have spoken is at its most acute. In our intermediate constitution the legislature is not subordinate to a sovereign text, as are the legislatures in 'constitutional' systems. Parliament remains the sovereign legislator. It, and not a written constitution, bears the ultimate mantle of democracy in the State.

However, the view that the rationale for judicial deference is the need to respect the democratic authority of the elected arms of government has not gone without challenge. Part of the reason is the conferment by Lord Bingham of a democratic mantle on the courts: an initiative that, I think, serves only to destabilise the constitutional balance. In *A v Secretary of State*[22] (the Belmarsh internment case) he said:

> I do not in particular accept the [Attorney General's] distinction which he drew between democratic institutions and the courts. It is of course true that the judges in this country are not elected and are not answerable to Parliament. It is also of course true ... that Parliament, the executive and the courts have different functions. But the function of independent judges charged to interpret and apply the law is universally recognised as a cardinal feature of the modern democratic state, a cornerstone of the Rule of Law itself. The Attorney General is fully entitled to insist on the proper limits of judicial authority, but he is wrong to stigmatise judicial decision-making as in some way undemocratic.[23]

---

[16] *SS (Nigeria) v Secretary of State for the Home Department* [2014] 1 WLR 998, para 28.
[17] *Brown v Stott* [2003] 1 AC 681.
[18] *R v Lambert* [2002] QB 1112.
[19] *Poplar v Donoghue* [2002] QB 48.
[20] *Marcic v Thames Water Utilities Ltd* [2004] 2 AC 42.
[21] *R v Lichniak* [2003] 1 AC 903.
[22] *A v Secretary of State for the Home Department* [2004] UKHL 56.
[23] ibid [42].

With great respect to Lord Bingham, I think this is confusing and therefore unhelpful. Certainly there are important connections between the Rule of Law and democracy: I said in chapter 2 that our foundational principles – reason, fairness and the presumption of liberty – are the constitution's prophylactic against arbitrary, capricious law, and so are by no means in opposition to democratic government; on the contrary, they are the very guardians of democracy's integrity. But that is because they confine democracy – not because they are part of it. Lord Bingham seems to fall into the trap of supposing that if the legitimacy of a State institution – in this case the common law courts – is not derived from the ideal of democracy, the institution must be 'undemocratic' and therefore a bad thing: but the common law cannot be so condemned, and so he invests it with a democratic pedigree. It is a futile exercise: it attributes to democracy a monopoly of political wisdom. But democracy is not the only virtue of a civilised State.

Lord Bingham's reasoning, moreover, leaves one wondering what he means by 'democracy'. It must be something beyond the principle of government elected on a universal franchise: the judges are not elected at all; but what could the intended meaning be? If the meaning of democracy is obscured, and the supposed virtue of democracy (whatever it means) is attributed to courts and government alike, the constitutional balance is destabilised because the two moralities, of law and politics, become confused; and the basis on which the law brings foundational principles to bear on government is undermined.

Lord Bingham's dictum in the Belmarsh case has, I think, encouraged Professor Allan to reject the straightforward proposition that judicial deference is due to the democratic arms of the State because of the authority the franchise confers. He espouses[24] the dictum of Lord Hoffmann in *ProLife*, which I have criticised, and he says this:

> There is ... no basis for any special deference to Parliament on the mere ground of its members' elected status: a representative body is as fully capable of infringing basic rights as any other; and the court's duty is to interpret its enactments (as far as possible) consistently with those rights, even if that interpretation departs significantly from 'ordinary' meaning. In the Belmarsh internment case ... Lord Bingham explicitly repudiated the idea of deference based on the court's unelected membership ...[25]

And Professor Allan proceeds to quote part of the passage from Lord Bingham's judgment that I have discussed.

Allan is of course right to say that a representative body is as well able as any other to violate basic rights. I was myself at pains in chapter 2 to emphasise that a representative democracy is fully capable of denying justice and right to unpopular people. Allan's concern, I think – one of his chief concerns – is that to acknowledge a discretionary area of judgement enjoyed by government on democratic grounds

---

[24] Allen (n 13) 269.
[25] ibid 273.

may create a field of public decision-making that would be immune from judicial review: 'the danger that a doctrine of deference will collapse in practice into a doctrine of non-justiciability',[26] and this, of course, would be thoroughly inimical to the Rule of Law and the constitutional balance.

But the doctrine of deference, at least as I would articulate it, is more nuanced than to give rise to such a risk. In *International Transport Roth GmbH* I sought to describe four principles that condition the application of judicial deference. I have already set out the first.[27] The second was that there is more scope for deference 'where the [European Convention on Human Rights] requires a balance to be struck, much less so where the right is stated in terms which are unqualified'.[28] The third and fourth principles were as follows:

> 85. The third principle is that greater deference will be due to the democratic powers where the subject-matter in hand is peculiarly within their constitutional responsibility, and less when it lies more particularly within the constitutional responsibility of the courts. The first duty of government is the defence of the realm. It is well settled that executive decisions dealing directly with matters of defence, while not immune from judicial review (that would be repugnant to the Rule of Law), cannot sensibly be scrutinised by the courts on grounds relating to their factual merits ... The first duty of the courts is the maintenance of the Rule of Law. That is exemplified in many ways, not least by the extremely restrictive construction always placed on no-certiorari clauses.
>
> ...
>
> 87. The fourth and last principle is very closely allied to the third, and indeed may be regarded as little more than an emanation of it; but I think it makes for clarity if it is separately articulated. It is that greater or lesser deference will be due according to whether the subject-matter lies more readily within the actual or potential expertise of the democratic powers or the courts. Thus, quite aside from defence, government decisions in the area of macro-economic policy will be relatively remote from judicial control: see for example *Ex p Nottinghamshire CC* [1986] AC 240 and *Ex p Hammersmith and Fulham LBC* [1991] 1 AC 521.

(I considered the *Nottinghamshire* case in chapter 5.) I do not think these observations were contradicted by the majority in *International Transport Roth GmbH* (Simon Brown and Jonathan Parker LJJ).

There are no doubt some cases – a diminishing class – of public decisions where the courts have no control. Article 9 of the Bill of Rights 1689 is an important constitutional constraint. And we have not reached the point where the Prime Minister's appointment of members of the government might be subject to judicial review. On the other hand, we have seen the extension of judicial review into the territory of the Royal prerogative.[29] The overall point I was seeking to make

---

[26] ibid 274.
[27] *International Transport Roth GmbH* (n 7) para 83.
[28] ibid para 84, citing Lord Hope in *Kebilene*.
[29] See ch 4: the cases of *GCHQ* and *Bentley*.

in the *Roth* case was that the application of judicial deference is case-sensitive; it does not involve the construction of rigid no-go areas; it is, quintessentially, a matter of degree according to the subject matter. Professor Allan refers to my approach to deference, saying:

> Laws LJ's various principles of deference exemplify the problematic nature of such doctrine, offering generalizations as a substitute for reasoning more finely tuned to the facts of individual cases.[30]

Perhaps I might be forgiven for saying that in describing principles 3 and 4 I thought I was acknowledging the very importance of the facts of individual cases. The important point, however, is that the nuance of particular circumstances is perfectly consistent with the application of overall principle, and judicial respect for the judgement on public issues of the elected arms of government is an important principle: it is the essence of what we have been calling judicial deference. I claim no particular wisdom for what I said in *Roth*; there are no doubt many ways of expressing the factors that militate in favour of a greater or lesser degree of judicial deference. But however precisely expressed, considerations of this kind show the constitutional balance at work.

I assume it to be elementary that the citizens of a democratic polity do not wish to be governed by unelected judges. That perfectly basic circumstance implies the imperative of judicial deference. More than this: the power of judicial review, which is vital to the Rule of Law, depends on such an acknowledgement. The judges, thankfully, have no tanks to roll onto other people's lawns. Sir Gerard Brennan, Chief Justice of the High Court of Australia from 1995 to 1998, said this in a lecture at University College Dublin on 22 April 1997:

> Having no power but the power of judgment, the Judiciary has no power base but public confidence in its integrity and competence in performing the functions assigned to it. There must be such a degree of public confidence in the courts' application of the law that neither power nor riches, nor political office nor numerical superiority can stand against the weight of the court's authority.[31]

Public confidence in the courts would not be enhanced by a diminished judicial respect for the authority of the ballot-box. It requires the principle of judicial deference, however nuanced and partial. Without it, the courts would lack the authority to fulfil their constitutional duty to uphold the Rule of Law by imposing on government and other public bodies the discipline of reason, fairness and the presumption of liberty.

For these reasons the discretionary area of judgement the courts allow to the elected arms of government is not merely dictated, as Allan would have it, 'by analysis of the substantive legal issues arising'.[32] The authority of the ballot-box is

---

[30] Allan (n 13) 272, fn 110.
[31] Sir Gerard Brennan CJ, 'The Third Branch and the Fourth Estate', second lecture in a series on Broadcasting, Society and the Law.
[32] Allan (n 13) 268.

a distinctive, free-standing and important factor in the courts' approach to judicial review of administrative action.

As I said at the beginning, deference and the creative use of statutory interpretation condition the courts' duty in any given case to find the edge or limit of statutory public power. It is a the duty that takes us back to chapter 1, and the way in which independent adjudication lifts the Rule of Law above the thin theory. The first, deference, pulls in favour of democratic power and the utilitarian morality of government. The second, creative interpretation, pulls in favour of constitutional principle and the Kantian morality of the common law. The bite or force of each – deference on the one hand, creative interpretation on the other – will be influenced by other factors having to do with the circumstances of the case. But this very fact, this flexibility, enriches the search for the edge or limit by means of the gradual, evolutive quality of the common law, enhanced and given effect by the law's fourfold methodology. I described these in chapter 4. And this, under our constitutional arrangements, is how the constitutional balance is achieved and maintained day to day.

Nothing in what I have said makes poodles of the judges. There is simply a constitutional need for judicial restraint when the courts venture onto the territory of the morality of government. But even among the qualified political rights given by Articles 8–11 of the European Convention, there are features that require a muscular judicial approach. In particular freedom of expression, guaranteed by Article 10, is a right that is inherent in the autonomy of the individual, the very basis of the morality of law. It is integral to one of the law's core principles – the presumption of liberty – and to the mandatory characteristics of the good constitution – difference and disputation – in short pluralism. Its preservation and encouragement therefore needs the special protection of the judges, and is critical to the constitutional balance. This is what gives free expression its central constitutional importance. I return to it in chapter 9.

7

Two Mistakes: Parliamentary Intent and the *Ultra Vires* Doctrine

As I said in the Introduction, the refutation both of the notion of parliamentary intent and of the *ultra vires* theory of judicial review is critical to the recognition and establishment of the constitutional balance. Both are central to an appreciation of the authority the constitutional fundamentals possess, and therefore to a proper understanding of the place of the constitutional balance. Both undermine vital pillars of the constitution – reason, fairness and the presumption of liberty – because they deliver them to the whim of the legislators for the time being. They open the door to the false notion that the democratic power is, in principle at least, untrammelled by fundamental standards – the mere creature of the legislative majority. But the constitution's pillars, fundamental standards, ought to be *integral* to the legislative process, not added on to it (or excluded from it) at the discretion of the legislature. This is a condition of the constitutional balance.

I. The Intention of Parliament

I shall start with the intention of Parliament. The integration of constitutional principles into the legislative function itself has been hindered and inhibited by this conception. That is so even though judges and others speak of it all the time. The intention of Parliament is seen as the key to the interpretation of statutes. Indeed, the interpretation of statutes is thought to *consist* in ascertaining the intention of Parliament. But in my view this language, this concept, is misleading and unhelpful. It has been a significant wrong turning in the development of our political philosophy. There is no such thing as the intention of Parliament. I shall explain why.

Scepticism about the idea of parliamentary intent is by no means new. Dworkin and Waldron have both had things to say on the subject. I shall not pretend that everything in what follows is original, though I hope some of it is. It is partly a philosophical treatise with more than a whiff of ordinary language philosophy, but I think it is necessary in order to get to the root of the matter; and I make no apology for that.

Parliament is a many-headed body. Intention is a characteristic of a single mind. The members of a group of persons may in theory have the *same* intention, in the sense that each may intend to act in the same way as each of the others. Or each may intend that he or she and all of the others should together act to achieve a common plan. But all of these cases are merely instances of members of the group individually intending the same result as each of the others. In neither circumstance does the group (as a whole) entertain an intention in the paradigm sense, that is, a state of mind of a single individual. A group does not have a mind, and therefore cannot possess a state of mind.

A. The Type-Token Distinction

This difference between a group each of whose members intends the same result as each of the others and an individual who entertains a single intention is of some importance. It calls to mind two meanings of the term 'the same'. Consider these two statements:

(a) 'They were all wearing the same raincoat.'
(b) 'They were all caught in the same thunderstorm.'

In proposition (a) there were many raincoats, but they all happened to be of the same design from Marks & Spencer. But in proposition (b) there was only one thunderstorm. Yet the use of the adjective 'same' is proper and correct in both propositions. It is just that the word 'same' can mean two different things – (i) where there is a single entity affecting many individuals – the same thunderstorm; and (ii) where there are many entities, which, however, may be said to be identical – the same raincoats.

The notion of parliamentary intent pretends to be a thunderstorm: the intention of a single entity, in the shape of the legislature. But it cannot work: a single intention can only be the possession of a single person. The intentions of our legislators can, at best, only be raincoats.

But that cannot work either. While it is logically possible for every member of the legislature to entertain the same intention as every other with respect to a Bill before Parliament, in the real world it never happens (save in a very etiolated sense to which I shall come shortly). First, there are all the Members of Parliament (MPs) and Members of the House of Lords who voted against the Bill. As for the possibility that every MP and every peer voted for the Bill, I am not a good enough historian to know when, if ever, there was unanimity in both Houses for proposed legislation. I would think never. Second, it is highly likely (and I imagine happens often in practice) that among MPs who vote in favour of a Bill there are differences of view as to what it will achieve and what precisely it means – some, with great respect to our elected representatives, may not have thought very deeply, or at all, about the latter question.

B. Can Parliamentary Intention be Saved? (1)

There is, however, one sense in which it may be said that, in respect of any Bill before Parliament, all the individual legislators are raincoats – they all share the same intention. This is elaborated in a book on the subject, *The Nature of Legislative Intent*, by Richard Ekins of St John's College Oxford.[1] Ekins' critical focus is on the idea that a group may act on a joint intention: that is, an intention to form and execute a joint plan of action. This is of course raincoats not thunderstorms. His idea is described in slightly varying ways at different points, notably in chapter 8, which is itself headed 'The Nature of Legislative Intent'. Thus Ekins says '[t]he legislature intends (its standing intention is) to choose to adopt proposals that are put before it and for which a majority of its members vote';[2] he refers to 'the plan or proposal that is held in common by all legislators and which explains the joint action';[3] then this:

> the standing intention of the legislature is to form, consider, and adopt law-making proposals, such that on majority vote the legislature acts on the relevant proposal … [t]he legislature's intention in any particular lawmaking act – the legislative intent – is to change the law in the complex, reasoned way set out in the open proposal for legislative action.[4]

Ekins' formulations are probably the best that can be done for the concept of parliamentary intent. The difficulty with it is that it is true but trivial. It says no more than that MPs intend to participate in the legislative process according to the rules. No doubt that is so; but if that is the best that can be done with the supposed notion of parliamentary intent, it is barren and useless, for it offers no guide whatever to the process of statutory interpretation, which was the only point of getting into the idea of parliamentary intent in the first place.

C. Can Parliamentary Intention be Saved? (2)

Perhaps the advocates of parliamentary intention can do better than this. They may have to accept that there are at most only raincoats and certainly no thunderstorm, but perhaps the raincoats are not limited to the anodyne truth that MPs intend to participate in the legislative process according to the rules. Perhaps they have more to say. Perhaps they can claim that at least the subjective intentions of the promoters of a Bill in Parliament can, if the Bill is passed and subject to all applicable amendments and qualifications, be said to represent the intention of Parliament as to what the Bill means.

---

[1] R Ekins, *The Nature of Legislative Intent* (Oxford University Press, 2012).
[2] ibid 230.
[3] ibid 231.
[4] ibid 242–43.

But this is hopeless. I shall come to the case of *Pepper v Hart* very shortly. But first – in principle – why should the Bill's promoters be the sole representatives of the intention of *Parliament*? What about other MPs who supported the Bill? As I have suggested, it is surely highly likely that the supporters of any Bill will have mixed motives and intentions, some more moved by the party whips than anything else. What about MPs who opposed the Bill, or abstained? The intention of the legislature is presumably supposed to be the intention of the legislature as a whole: the intention of *Parliament*, not the intention of this or that MP.

Parliamentary intention, then, even if you allow raincoats though there is no thunderstorm, remains elusive except in Ekins' etiolated and uninteresting sense: MPs intend to participate in the legislative process according to the rules: true but trivial. Any attempt to give the idea a deeper and more useful meaning, relevant to the business of construing statutes, founders on two rocks: (i) the type-token distinction – the so-called intention of Parliament can only be raincoats; (ii) even if you are prepared to buy the raincoats, the many heads of Parliament will not all share the same subjective intention to put the Bill on the statute book with a meaning understood by all to be the same: as I said earlier, in the real world it never happens. So there are not even raincoats.

i. Pepper v Hart

None of this troubled their Lordships in *Pepper v Hart*,[5] in which, as is well known, the House of Lords permitted (in limited circumstances) the ascertainment of so-called parliamentary intent, as a guide to construction, by reference to what was said in Parliament by the promoters of the Bill in question. The importance of parliamentary intent was taken as a given. Lord Browne-Wilkinson said this:

> In my judgment, subject to the questions of the privileges of the House of Commons, reference to Parliamentary material should be permitted as an aid to the construction of legislation which is ambiguous or obscure or the literal meaning of which leads to an absurdity. Even in such cases references in court to Parliamentary material should only be permitted where such material clearly discloses the mischief aimed at or the legislative intention lying behind the ambiguous or obscure words. In the case of statements made in Parliament, as at present advised I cannot foresee that any statement other than the statement of the Minister or other promoter of the Bill is likely to meet these criteria ... Statute law consists of the words that Parliament has enacted. It is for the courts to construe those words and it is the court's duty in so doing to give effect to the intention of Parliament in using those words ...[6]

---

[5] *Pepper v Hart* [1993] AC 593.
[6] ibid 634D–F.

I should also note this citation from Lord Griffiths, which, as I shall try to show, begins to point the way out of the trap of intention, though his Lordship is still caught in its claws:

> The object of the court in interpreting legislation is to give effect so far as the language permits to the intention of the legislature. If the language proves to be ambiguous I can see no sound reason not to consult Hansard to see if there is a clear statement of the meaning that the words were intended to carry. The days have long passed when the courts adopted a strict constructionist view of interpretation which required them to adopt the literal meaning of the language. The courts now adopt a purposive approach which seeks to give effect to the true purpose of legislation and are prepared to look at much extraneous material that bears upon the background against which the legislation was enacted. Why then cut ourselves off from the one source in which may be found an authoritative statement of the intention with which the legislation is placed before Parliament?[7]

Note Lord Griffiths' use of the term *purpose* – 'the true purpose of legislation' – as well as *intention*. He appears to use them interchangeably; but in my opinion the difference is very important, and I shall return to it.

Pepper v Hart has been criticised since, notably by Lord Steyn in his article 'Pepper v Hart: a Re-examination',[8] and by Lord Hoffmann in *Robinson v Secretary of State for Northern Ireland*.[9] A principal element in these criticisms has been the contention that the use of material from parliamentary debates, to the extent authorised by *Pepper v Hart*, has made the law more inaccessible and litigation more expensive. Here is Lord Hoffmann in the *Robinson* case:

> References to Hansard are now fairly frequently included in argument and beneath those references there must lie a large spoil heap of material which has been mined in the course of research without yielding anything worthy even of a submission ...[10]

But these practical considerations, important as they no doubt are, do not in my opinion get to the root of the matter. To my mind the true defect in the decision in *Pepper v Hart*, and the root objection to the notion of parliamentary intent (beyond the thunderstorm and the raincoats) is as I have described it: the deployment of parliamentary intent as a primary tool – certainly if it is *the* primary tool – of statutory construction undermines vital pillars of the constitution: reason, fairness and the presumption of liberty, because it delivers them to the whim of the legislators for the time being. The *ultra vires* doctrine of judicial review (to which I shall come shortly), indirectly at least, has similar effects.

Some insight into the negative consequences of the notion of parliamentary intent is to be gained from a comparison between the interpretation of contracts and of statutes, to which I shall now briefly turn.

---

[7] ibid 617B–C.
[8] Lord Steyn, 'Pepper v Hart: a Re-examination' (2001) 21 *OJLS* 59.
[9] *Robinson v Secretary of State for Northern Ireland* [2002] UKHL 32 [39]–[40].
[10] ibid [40].

ii. Interpreting Contracts and Statutes

I have noted Lord Griffiths' apparently interchangeable use of the terms *intention* and *purpose*. Now it might be thought that this does not matter very much: however valid my criticisms of parliamentary intention strictly so called – the thunderstorm and the raincoats – what their Lordships in *Pepper v Hart* were getting at was the ascertainment of the Act's purpose, and that is unquestionably a major function of statutory interpretation; the slippage between the language of intention and the language of purpose is in truth, so the argument would go, no more than a matter of semantics.

But the difference between intent and purpose is, as I have said, very important. Consider the respective functions of interpreting contracts and interpreting statutes. The point of the former *is* to ascertain the *intention* of the parties. The point of the latter is to ascertain the *purpose* of the Act. Although the construction of contracts (i) eschews any overt enquiry into the subjective intention of the contracting parties and (ii) looks to the 'natural and ordinary meaning' of the words used, both of those propositions are interestingly qualified in Lord Hoffmann's well-known exposition in the *Investors Compensation Scheme* case in 1997.[11] Here are two of his five core principles:

> (3) The law excludes from the admissible background the previous negotiations of the parties and their declarations of subjective intent. They are admissible only in an action for rectification. The law makes this distinction for reasons of practical policy and, in this respect only, legal interpretation differs from the way we would interpret utterances in ordinary life ...

> (5) The 'rule' that words should be given their 'natural and ordinary meaning' reflects the common sense proposition that we do not easily accept that people have made linguistic mistakes, particularly in formal documents. On the other hand, if one would nevertheless conclude from the background that something must have gone wrong with the language, the law does not require judges to attribute to the parties an intention which they plainly could not have had ...[12]

I think it is implicit in this reasoning, and it is no doubt anyway obvious, that the purpose of construing a contract is indeed to ascertain what the parties intended. Unlike the many-headed legislature, at least in the paradigm case the individual parties to a contract will indeed intend this or that specific result when they enter into the contract: intend in the ordinary sense. Of course there are many-headed contracts. Each party to a contract is a distinct legal person. A corporate party will have a controlling mind; a natural person will have his or her own mind. Direct enquiry into subjective intent is, it is true, generally excluded, but that is 'for reasons of practical policy' – including, no doubt, the avoidance of protracted and uncertain litigation. The contract's natural and ordinary meaning is given primacy, but that is defeasible if 'something must have gone wrong'.

---

[11] *Investors Compensation Scheme v West Bromwich Building Society* [1998] 1 WLR 896.
[12] ibid 913B–E.

This brings us to the difference – the important difference – between construing contracts and construing statutes. As every first-year law student knows, the general rule is that a contract only binds the parties to it, though obviously it may have important effects and consequences for third parties. Interpreting a contract gives effect to the rights and duties it confers and imposes on the parties to it. Subject to cases of fraud, undue influence or overriding public policy, the court's only concern is to see that those rights and duties are properly distributed in accordance with the parties' actual intention expressed in the contract. That intention is both real and paramount.

By contrast, interpreting a statute – a Public General Act – gives effect to rights and duties imposed by the legislature on citizens and the State at large. It is an instrument of government. The affected citizen was obviously not a party to the Act; he or she will have had no say – no direct say – as to what went into the Bill on its way through Parliament. And the State itself has many faces and functions, not all of which will have had any more say as to what should go into the Bill than had the citizen. The interest of parties to a contract in the contract's correct construction is, *entirely*, to see their intentions vindicated (I leave aside, of course, any discussion of the parties' *motives*, which is quite a different matter). The principal interest of citizen and State in a statute's correct construction is to see that the statute fulfils a clear and proper governmental purpose within a proper constitutional framework, and to identify what that purpose is.

D. Intent and Purpose

The essential point here is that whereas the construction of a contract is an exercise devoted only to the ascertainment of its makers' intention, the interpretation of a statute involves more than the ascertainment of its purpose. The statute's construction also involves the application of our constitutional principles, which the Rule of Law imposes on the process of legislation. The problem with the idea of parliamentary intent – quite aside from the thunderstorm and the raincoats – is that it looks like the whole story: the only begetter of the statute's meaning. As a tool of interpretation the intention of Parliament tends to subsume within itself the constitutional principles that qualify and moderate the meaning of the statute in question, so that those principles are the creation, not of the constitution, but of the legislators from time to time. If instead we speak of the purpose of the statute rather than the intention of the legislature, we shall avoid such a trap; or at least we shall be less likely to fall into it.

E. An Irony

Before leaving the contrast between statutes and contracts, let me draw attention to what seems to me to be an irony arising out of the comparison between the two. We have seen that in relation to contracts, as Lord Hoffmann said, 'the law excludes from the admissible background the previous negotiations of the parties and their declarations of subjective intent'. But in relation to statutes, when the *Pepper v Hart* approach is applied, the law admits express declarations of intent – the intent of the Minister proposing the Bill. So in a context where the true purpose of interpretation is to find out the parties' intent – contracts – direct evidence of that intent is excluded; but where the true purpose of interpretation is (on my approach) to discover not intent but purpose, direct evidence of intent is in fact admitted. Something has gone wrong. The error at the root of it lies in treating statutory construction as a search for intention.

F. The Constitutional Principles

Let me say a further word about the place of the constitutional principles. Our constitutional law requires that the construction of a statute, to the extent that it distributes rights and duties between citizen and State, is shaped by the application of constitutional principles that are independent of anything that could be called parliamentary intent. As I have said, the core principles are very familiar: reason, fairness and the presumption of liberty. I have already discussed them at length in chapter 5. As we have seen, these principles are imposed on the functions of the State, including the framing of primary legislation, by the Rule of Law, for without them government would be arbitrary and capricious and worse. They colour and direct the construction of statutes. Being constitutional principles they cannot be the creature of the legislature's intention (were there such a thing), which changes at the choice of the legislators from time to time, even day by day. They are the constitutional balance at work.

If it is possible, the Rule of Law and the traditional English doctrine of legislative supremacy should lie in the same bed. The concept of parliamentary intention impedes such an outcome. The concept of a statute's purpose does not. Our constitutional principles – in particular the three I have emphasised – apply to statutes generally, and are separate and distinct from the specific purpose of any particular statute, though the general principles and the specific purpose have to live together.

II. The *Ultra Vires* Doctrine

The *ultra vires* doctrine purports to state the *source* – the ultimate legal source – of the judicial review power to set the standards that take the Rule of Law past the thin theory (for which see chapter 1). It says that the source of the power is Parliament – the legislature. I do not agree. It implies the truth of parliamentary intent, which I have sought to contradict, and suffers from other defects.

For some years there has been an energetic debate in academic circles upon the question whether the *ultra vires* doctrine is indeed the constitutional foundation of judicial review. The subject has acquired a substantial literature, to the extent that not a few academics would nowadays regard it as old hat; but it is important to be clear about it in order to be clear about the constitutional balance. The subject is very thoroughly covered in the essays contained in *Judicial Review and the Constitution*[13] ('the *Essays*'), edited by Professor Christopher Forsyth. In his first contribution to the *Essays*, 'Ultra Vires and the Foundations of Judicial Review' (first published in 1998[14]), Professor Paul Craig expresses the 'core idea' of *ultra vires* as follows: 'The *ultra vires* principle is based on the assumption that judicial review is legitimated on the ground that the courts are applying the intent of the legislature.'[15] In other words, the will of Parliament is the source of the judicial review jurisdiction.

A. The Nature of the *Ultra Vires* Doctrine

I shall not take time repeating the criticisms of the notion of parliamentary intent that I have just advanced. There are other points to be made. In a major article published early in the *ultra vires* debate,[16] Professor Christopher Forsyth describes and defends the doctrine in this way:

> [W]hat an all-powerful Parliament does not prohibit, it must authorise either expressly or impliedly. Likewise if Parliament grants a power to a Minister, that Minister either acts within those powers or outside those powers. There is no grey area between author-isation and the denial of power. Thus, if the making of vague regulations is within the powers granted by a sovereign Parliament, on what basis may the courts challenge Parliament's will and hold that the regulations are invalid? If Parliament has author-ised vague regulations, those regulations cannot be challenged without challenging Parliament's authority to authorise such regulations ...
>
> The upshot of this is that ... one is led inevitably to the conclusion that to abandon *ultra vires* is to challenge the supremacy of Parliament.[17]

Earlier[18] Professor Forsyth had cited a passage from an article of mine,[19] in which I said this:

> [It] cannot be suggested that all these principles [viz. the modern principles of judicial review] ... were suddenly interwoven into the legislature's intentions in the 1960s and 70s and onward, in which period they have been articulated and enforced by the courts. They are, categorically, judicial creations. They owe neither their existence nor their acceptance to the will of the legislature. They have nothing to do with the intention of Parliament, save as a fig leaf to cover their true origins. We do not need the fig leaf any more.

---

[13] C Forsyth (ed), *Judicial Review and the Constitution* (Hart Publishing, 2000).

[14] P Craig, 'Ultra Vires and the Foundations of Judicial Review' (1998) 57(1) *CLJ* 63.

[15] P Craig, 'Ultra Vires and the Foundations of Judicial Review' in *Essays* (n 13) ch 3, 48.

[16] C Forsyth, 'Of Fig Leaves and Fairy Tales: the Ultra Vires Doctrine, the Sovereignty of Parliament and Judicial Review' [1996] *CLJ* 122 (see also *Essays* (n 13) ch 2, 29).

[17] Forsyth, *Essays* (n 13) 39–40.

[18] ibid 34.

[19] Sir John Laws, 'Law and Democracy' [1995] *PL* 72, 79.

These observations of mine, and the views of some others, evoked a very strong response from Professor Forsyth. He said:

> [I]n a democratic polity change in the constitutional order must – or at any rate should – come about through the democratic process. And the judiciary, as important as its independence is to the Rule of Law, is a non-elected part of the constitutional order. How can some judges suppose they are entitled to change the fundamentals of the constitution without reference to the elected elements of that constitution? ... The attack by some judges on the doctrine of ultra vires and the sovereignty of Parliament is but the latest example of judges missing their footing on [the constitutional] bedrock. It is to be hoped that it is the last.[20]

I shall turn next to the substantive objections to the *ultra vires* doctrine.

B. Objections to the *Ultra Vires* Doctrine

The formulation of the *ultra vires* rule in the unqualified form given by Professor Craig – '[t]he *ultra vires* principle is based on the assumption that judicial review is legitimated on the ground that the courts are applying the intent of the legislature' – is, taken literally, no more than a legal fiction. Parliament did not legislate so as to require the courts to institute the *Wednesbury* doctrine, or the duty to hear the other side, or any aspect of the presumption of liberty. Consider this passage from Craig's 1998 article:

> Let us imagine that ... the UK courts were to decide in 1998 that proportionality was an independent head of review. Can it plausibly be maintained that this is to be justified by reference to changes in legislative intent which occurred at this time? Would the legislature in some manner have indicated that it intended a new generalised head of review which had not existed before? The question only has to be posed for the answer to be self-evident ...[21]

Thus (as I indicated in chapter 4) it is surely implausible to suppose that Parliament intended that the ouster clause in *Anisminic* should be as limited in effect as the House of Lords held. Moreover, as has often been pointed out, the judicial review jurisdiction is by no means only directed at the exercise of discretionary power conferred by Act of Parliament. As we saw, again in chapter 4, it may encompass decisions made under the Royal Prerogative.[22] It is also deployed to control acts of non-governmental bodies exercising what the court deems to be public functions: the Take-over Panel was an example in 1987.[23] Obviously in such cases the source of the jurisdiction cannot be the intent of the legislature.

---

[20] Forsyth, *Essays* (n 13) 46.
[21] Craig (n 14) 68.
[22] *CCSU v Minister for the Civil Service* [1985] AC 374 ('*GCHQ*'); *R v Home Secretary, ex parte Bentley* [1994] QB 349.
[23] *R v Panel on Take-overs and Mergers, ex parte Datafin plc* [1987] 2 WLR 699.

We can see, then, that the proposition that judicial review is itself a creature of Parliament's intention is effectively contradicted by some of the leading modern authority, as well as by the essential incoherence of the very notion of parliamentary intent, which I sought to expose earlier. Nor can it be saved by any appeal to the history of judicial review. As Craig says, '[w]e must ... look to the prerogative writs in order to understand the foundations of judicial review'.[24] This is followed in Craig's article by a discussion[25] of the writs of mandamus, certiorari and prohibition, which I will not summarise here[26] but which demonstrates that the disciplines they enforced were not seen as creatures of legislative intent: in a later essay Craig notes that '[f]or Coke, Holt and Mansfield the central idea was the capacity of the common law to control governmental and non-governmental power'.[27]

Forsyth's reply to Craig's appeal to legal history is as follows:

> [I]t is no reply ... to point, as Professor Craig does, to ancient cases which, he claims, did not have regard to the intent of the legislature in imposing standards upon decision-making bodies. These decisions antedate the development of our sovereign Parliament in its modern form and the current question simply did not arise in this way in those days.[28]

But this is no answer. Craig is discussing the jurisdictional foundation of judicial review: the constitutional or legal source of the judicial review power. It originated in the royal power exercised through the Court of King's Bench. Its source did not suddenly switch with the advent of the doctrine of Parliamentary sovereignty after the upheavals of the seventeenth century.

C. Modified *Ultra Vires*

Faced with these and other criticisms, the defenders of *ultra vires*, notably Professors Elliott[29] and Forsyth,[30] have developed a modified version of the theory. It is expressed by Professor Elliott thus:

> [W]hen Parliament enacts legislation which (typically) confers wide discretionary power and which makes no explicit reference to the controls which should regulate

---

[24] Craig (n 14) 80.

[25] ibid 81–86.

[26] See Craig's collection of references in Craig (n 14) 81, fn 47.

[27] Forsyth (n 13) 389.

[28] C Forsyth, 'Heat and Light: A Plea for Reconciliation' in *Essays* (n 13) 393, 399.

[29] M Elliott, 'The Demise of Parliamentary Sovereignty? The Implications for Justifying Judicial Review' (1999) 115 LQR 119; M Elliott, 'The Ultra Vires Doctrine in a Constitutional Setting: Still the Central Principle of Administrative Law' [1999] *CLJ* 129; M Elliott, *The Constitutional Foundations of Judicial Review* (Oxford University Press, 2001); *Beatson, Matthews and Elliott's Administrative Law, Text and Materials*, 4th edn (Oxford University Press, 2011).

[30] Forsyth (n 16).

the exercise of the power, the courts are constitutionally entitled ... to assume that it was Parliament's intention to legislate in conformity with the Rule of Law principle ... Parliament must be taken to withhold from decision-makers the power to treat individuals in a manner which offends the Rule of Law: for this reason, the competence to act unfairly and unreasonably should be assumed to be absent from any parliamentary grant. However, the task of transforming this general intention – that the executive should respect the Rule of Law – into detailed, legally enforceable rules of fairness and rationality is clearly a matter for the courts, through the incremental methodology of the forensic process ... [The modified ultra vires theory] recognizes that the constitutional order itself locates the legislature and the legislation which it passes within a framework which is founded on the Rule of Law, and which therefore at*tributes to the legislature an intention to act consistently with that principle.*[31]

Professor Forsyth is likewise at pains to emphasise that the modified *ultra vires* theory does not entail an attribution to the will of Parliament of all the evolving principles of review developed by the judges:

It does not assert that every nuance of every ground of judicial review is to be found in the implied intent of the legislature ... It simply asserts that when the courts do turn to common law principle to guide their development of judicial review they are doing what Parliament intended them to do.[32]

Forsyth asserts that in four decisions of the House of Lords[33] 'the leading speeches clearly favour the modified *ultra vires* doctrine (or something very similar)'.[34] But some of the statements relied on are by no means clear support for Professor Forsyth's position. Let me give two short examples. In *Ex parte Pierson* Lord Steyn said:

[Parliament] legislates for a European liberal democracy founded on the principles and traditions of the common law and the courts may approach legislation on this initial assumption.[35]

And in the same case Lord Browne-Wilkinson stated:

A power conferred by Parliament in general terms is not to be taken to authorise the doing of acts by the donee of the power which adversely affects the legal rights of the citizen or the basic principles on which the law of the United Kingdom is based unless the statute makes it clear that such was the intention of the Parliament.[36]

However, the proposition that Parliament legislates consistently with the common law, or does not authorise violations of common law principles, does not entail the

---

[31] Elliott, *The Constitutional Foundations of Judicial Review* (n 29) (cited in *Beatson, Matthews and Elliott's Administrative Law* (n 29) 21).

[32] Forsyth (n 28) 397.

[33] *R v Secretary of State for the Home Department, ex parte Pierson* [1998] AC 539; *Boddington v British Transport Police* [1999] 2 AC 143; *R v Lord President of the Privy Council, ex parte Page* [1993] AC 682; *R v Secretary of State for the Home Department, ex parte Abdi* [1996] 1 WLR 298.

[34] Forsyth (n 28) 397.

[35] *Ex parte Pierson* (n 33) 587C–D.

[36] ibid 575D.

further proposition that Parliament is the constitutional source of the legal power to make those principles. It means only that legislation is to be construed consistently with common law principle unless there is clear provision to the contrary.

D. Shortcomings of the Modified Theory

The sharpest articulation of the modified *ultra vires* theory is perhaps that given by Professor Forsyth: 'when the courts do turn to common law principle to guide their development of judicial review they are doing what Parliament intended them to do'. Here, then, *ultra vires* is seen directly as the child of parliamentary intention, and it seems to me there is no escape from the criticisms I offered of the latter notion earlier in this chapter; they give the lie to the *ultra vires* theory as well as parliamentary intent itself.

What is actually meant by the proposition that in developing the principles of judicial review the courts are doing what Parliament intended them to do? It looks like a claim about statutory interpretation – that on the proper construction of this or that statute it will be seen that our fundamental principles, which are the flesh of judicial review, are inherent in the statute's meaning.

In the eye of the law, the concept of parliamentary intention only exists as a function of statutory interpretation. Therefore the ascertainment of Parliament's intention can only be a matter of statutory construction. Any broader view of legislative intent as a legal construct, let alone as a source of constitutional power, is incoherent, for Parliament's only means of expressing its intent is by legislation. And such a broader view, even if it could be coherently articulated, would lack democratic legitimacy: it would be difficult to see how it might be the fruit of any perceptible or recognisable democratic process.

But the *ultra vires* doctrine, which asserts an intention on the part of the legislature to confer the power of judicial review on the judges, cannot be found in any statute by means of any recognisable canon of interpretation. No Act of Parliament states such a proposition; nor is it to be inferred from the terms of any Act.

I think it is clear that the proponents of the *ultra vires* doctrine, in its original or modified form, do not in fact purport to derive the legislative intention they assert from the construction of any particular statute or statutes. The theory involves no exercise of statutory interpretation at all. It asserts a supposed principle, that Parliament has authorised the judicial review jurisdiction, but cannot point to any parliamentary source that suggests that Parliament has actually done so.

It may be objected that these criticisms are more apparent than real. Many rules of construction involve the imputation of a particular intention to Parliament that is by no means apparent from the terms of the statute in hand. The cases to which I referred in chapter 1 – the strict interpretation of criminal and taxing statutes, and the presumption against retrospectivity – may be said to be examples of such rules. Why should the imputation of an intent that the judges apply public law standards to discretionary decision-making not count as just such a rule?

The imputation of legislative intent in such cases as criminal statutes, etc is the means by which the common law courts impose particular standards on the execution of specific activities governed by statute. However, unless expressed in the statute, there is no basis for saying that they are the legislator's creature. Most often they are imposed by the courts – itself a recognition by the courts of constitutional principle. The purported derivation of our constitutional principles lock, stock and barrel from the supposed intention of Parliament is something else altogether.

If my refutation of Parliamentary intent and *ultra vires* is correct, there are obviously implications for the nature and scope of the sovereignty of Parliament. I shall turn to that next.

8

The Sovereignty of Parliament

The doctrine of Parliamentary supremacy[1] has in our legal history over some three hundred years been the leading article of faith in English constitutional law, described and to an extent established by AV Dicey in *The Law of the Constitution*.[2] The doctrine consists in two interlocking propositions, which I think may reasonably be articulated as follows:

(a) The Queen in Parliament may in the form of primary legislation pass any measure whatsoever (and so may overrule decisions of the courts).
(b) The courts and all other public authorities are bound to give effect to any measure so passed.

In recent years, however, the doctrine has been subjected to a degree of strain, the principal engines of which have been the law of the European Union (EU) and the law of human rights. I shall address some effects of European law before coming to the implications of the last chapter. I shall have more to say about human rights in chapter 9.

In the case of *Jackson*,[3] which concerned the legislation prohibiting hunting with hounds, Lord Steyn said this in the Supreme Court:

> 102. ... If the Attorney General is right the 1949 [Parliament] Act could also be used to introduce oppressive and wholly undemocratic legislation. For example, it could theoretically be used to abolish judicial review of flagrant abuse of power by a government or even the role of the ordinary courts in standing between the executive and citizens. This is where we may have to come back to the point about the supremacy of Parliament. We do not in the United Kingdom have an uncontrolled constitution as the Attorney General implausibly asserts. In the European context the second *Factortame* decision made that clear: [1991] 1 AC 603. The settlement contained in the Scotland Act 1998 also points to a divided sovereignty. Moreover, the European Convention on Human Rights as incorporated into our law by the Human Rights Act, 1998, created a new legal order. One must not assimilate the ECHR with multilateral treaties of the traditional type. Instead it is a legal order in which the United Kingdom assumes obligations to protect fundamental rights, not in relation to other states, but towards all

---

[1] The history and philosophy of legislative supremacy cannot sensibly be studied without recourse to J Goldsworthy, *The Sovereignty of Parliament: History and Philosophy* (Oxford University Press, 1999).
[2] AV Dicey, *The Study of the Law of the Constitution*, 1st edn (1885).
[3] *R (Jackson) v Attorney General* [2005] UKSC 56.

individuals within its jurisdiction. The classic account given by Dicey of the doctrine of the supremacy of Parliament, pure and absolute as it was, can now be seen to be out of place in the modern United Kingdom. Nevertheless, the supremacy of Parliament is still the *general* principle of our constitution. It is a construct of the common law. The judges created this principle. If that is so, it is not unthinkable that circumstances could arise where the courts may have to qualify a principle established on a different hypothesis of constitutionalism. In exceptional circumstances involving an attempt to abolish judicial review or the ordinary role of the courts, the Appellate Committee of the House of Lords or a new Supreme Court may have to consider whether this is a constitutional fundamental which even a sovereign Parliament acting at the behest of a complaisant House of Commons cannot abolish.

In the same case Lord Hope said this:

> 103. I start where my learned friend Lord Steyn has just ended. Our constitution is dominated by the sovereignty of Parliament. But Parliamentary sovereignty is no longer, if it ever was, absolute ... It is no longer right to say that its freedom to legislate admits of no qualification whatever. Step by step, gradually but surely, the English principle of the absolute legislative sovereignty of Parliament which Dicey derived from Coke and Blackstone is being qualified.

Against that the remarks of Lord Neuberger, President of the Supreme Court from 2012 to 2017, giving the Lord Alexander of Weedon Lecture in 2011, seem almost defensive:

> [E]ven the strongest advocate of limiting parliamentary authority must accept that the courts could only overrule parliament in wholly exceptional cases. Given the absence of a written constitution, it seems very hard to identify with clarity and consistency the circumstances in which the courts could take such a course. It is therefore difficult to see how there would be perceived legitimacy in the courts overruling parliament; and perceived legitimacy is of the essence where there is no written constitution.[4]

More specifically the doctrine has had to accommodate the seeming supremacy of European Union law. In *Factortame (No 1)*,[5] provisions made under the Merchant Shipping Act 1988 were held to be subject to rights guaranteed by EU law, which of course were effective in the United Kingdom (UK) by force of the earlier statute, the European Communities Act 1972. Lord Bridge said this:

> By virtue of section 2(4) of the Act of 1972 Part II of the Act of 1988 is to be construed and take effect subject to directly enforceable Community rights ... This has precisely the same effect as if a section were incorporated in Part II of the Act of 1988 which in terms enacted that the provisions with respect to registration of British fishing vessels were to be without prejudice to the directly enforceable Community rights of nationals of any member state of the EEC.[6]

---

[4] Lord Neuberger of Abbotsbury, MR, 'Who Are the Masters Now?', Second Lord Alexander of Weedon Lecture (6 April 2011) 5, para 16.
[5] *R v Secretary of State for Transport, ex parte Factortame Ltd (No 1)* [1990] 2 AC 85.
[6] ibid para 140.

I said in *Thoburn* (to which I have referred in passing in chapters 2 and 4) that '[i]t seems to me that there is no doubt but that in *Factortame (No 1)* the House of Lords effectively accepted that s 2(4) [ie of the 1972 Act] could not be impliedly repealed, albeit the point was not argued.'[7] That view, so far as I know, has not been contradicted.

I. Constitutional Statutes and Implied Repeal

The doctrine of implied repeal has for long been regarded as a mainstream element in the constitutional principle of Parliamentary sovereignty. The rule is that if Parliament has enacted successive statutes that, on the true construction of each of them, make irreducibly inconsistent provisions, the earlier statute is impliedly repealed by the later. The importance of the rule, on the traditional view, is that if it were otherwise, the earlier Parliament might bind the later, and this would be repugnant to the principle of Parliamentary sovereignty. But the rule has been modified in the face of EU power.

However, the doctrine of implied repeal was by no means abolished, and the sovereignty of Parliament was not ultimately compromised. Plainly the House of Lords did not decide in *Factortame (No 1)* that the European Communities Act (or any part of it) could not be *expressly* repealed. In *Thoburn*, I said this:

> 62. ... In the present state of its maturity the common law has come to recognise that there exist rights which should properly be classified as constitutional or fundamental: see for example such cases as *Simms* [2000] 2 AC 115 *per* Lord Hoffmann at 131, *Pierson v Secretary of State* [1998] AC 539, *Leech* [1994] QB 198, *Derbyshire County Council v Times Newspapers Ltd* [1993] AC 534, and *Witham* [1998] QB 575. And from this a further insight follows. We should recognise a hierarchy of Acts of Parliament: as it were 'ordinary' statutes and 'constitutional' statutes. The two categories must be distinguished on a principled basis. In my opinion a constitutional statute is one which (a) conditions the legal relationship between citizen and State in some general, over-arching manner, or (b) enlarges or diminishes the scope of what we would now regard as fundamental constitutional rights. (a) and (b) are of necessity closely related: it is difficult to think of an instance of (a) that is not also an instance of (b). The special status of constitutional statutes follows the special status of constitutional rights. Examples are the Magna Carta, the Bill of Rights 1689, the Act of Union, the Reform Acts which distributed and enlarged the franchise, the [Human Rights Act 1998] the Scotland Act 1998 and the Government of Wales Act 1998. The [European Communities Act] clearly belongs in this family. It incorporated the whole corpus of substantive Community rights and obligations, and gave overriding domestic effect to the judicial and administrative machinery of Community law. It may be there has never been a statute having such profound effects on so many dimensions of our daily lives. The [European Communities Act] is, by force of the common law, a constitutional statute.

---

[7] *Thoburn v Sunderland City Council* [2003] QB 151, para 61.

63. Ordinary statutes may be impliedly repealed. Constitutional statutes may not. For the repeal of a constitutional Act or the abrogation of a fundamental right to be effected by statute, the court would apply this test: is it shown that the legislature's *actual* – not imputed, constructive or presumed – intention was to effect the repeal or abrogation? I think the test could only be met by express words in the later statute, or by words so specific that the inference of an actual determination to effect the result contended for was irresistible. The ordinary rule of implied repeal does not satisfy this test. Accordingly, it has no application to constitutional statutes.

I have discussed the idea of constitutional statutes in *The UK Constitution after Miller: Brexit and Beyond*.[8] There I acknowledge that the notion of constitutional statutes poses practical challenges, demonstrated not least by Professor David Feldman's important and constructive criticisms.[9] The practicalities are particularly significant because although our membership of the EU may have furnished the context for the emergence of constitutional statutes, it by no means provided the limit or edge of their place in the long term. In *Thoburn*[10] I gave examples (the Magna Carta of 1215, the Bill of Rights of 1689, the Act of Union 1707 and others) of Acts of Parliament that are undoubtedly constitutional cornerstones, and which I would classify as constitutional statutes. Constitutional statutes were not a creature of our membership of the EU. It is of some interest to compare what was said by Lord Neuberger and Lord Mance in the *HS2* case:

> The United Kingdom has no written constitution, but we have a number of constitutional instruments. They include Magna Carta, the Petition of Right 1628, the Bill of Rights and (in Scotland) the Claim of Rights Act 1689, the Act of Settlement 1701 and the Act of Union 1707. The European Communities Act 1972, the Human Rights Act 1998 and the Constitutional Reform Act 2005 may now be added to this list. The common law itself also recognises certain principles as fundamental to the Rule of Law. It is, putting the point at its lowest, certainly arguable (and it is for United Kingdom law and courts to determine) that there may be fundamental principles, whether contained in other constitutional instruments or recognised at common law, of which Parliament when it enacted the European Communities Act 1972 did not either contemplate or authorise the abrogation.[11]

Professor Feldman offers three reasons for regarding the link I suggested at paragraph 62 of *Thoburn* as problematic.[12] The first is that the category of fundamental rights is not closed. The second is that some 'constitutional' legislation is not concerned with rights. The third is that the 'rights' aspect of my suggested test ('[a statute which] enlarges or diminishes the scope of what we would now

---

[8] Sir John Laws, 'The Miller Case and Constitutional Statutes' in M Elliott, J Williams and AL Young (eds), *The UK Constitution after Miller: Brexit and Beyond* (Hart Publishing, 2018) ch 9.

[9] D Feldman, 'The Nature and Significance of "Constitutional" Legislation' (2013) 129 *LQR* 343.

[10] *Thoburn* (n 7) para 62.

[11] *R (on the application of HS2 Action Alliance Ltd) v Secretary of State for Transport* [2014] UKSC 3, [2014] 1 WLR 324, [207].

[12] Feldman (n 9) 345.

regard as fundamental constitutional rights') is over-inclusive: '[m]ost legislation is concerned with the relationship between the state and citizens, in that it confers powers on state agencies to interfere with or regulate citizens' activities'.[13] All these points will enliven future debate. I shall not engage with them individually here, save to say that none of them refutes the proposition, obvious perhaps, that some statutes have far-reaching constitutional effects and others do not: a proposition that I think needs to be translated into an express hierarchy, however general.

For present purposes, however, I would underline this observation in Professor Feldman's conclusions: 'The important point is that we cannot systematically identify constitutional legislation without a notion of the central function or functions of constitutions'.[14] I suggested in chapter 4 that the core of a constitution is that set of laws, or laws and conventions, that in a sovereign State define the relationship between the ruler and the ruled. It must therefore include definitions of the ruler and the ruled, and of the powers and duties of each. Such a definition, or description, is ordinary enough; but it brings us directly back to the constitutional balance.

A perception of parliamentary sovereignty that treats every statute as having equal weight and value tends to exclude the idea of constitutional principle (other than the simple principle of the legislature's omnipotence) from the structure of legislation. It thereby distances the legislative process from the Rule of Law. This malign equality between Acts of Parliament may, however, be – and often is – shaken by robust judicial approaches to statutory interpretation. To treat some Acts as constitutional statutes may – should – be seen as just such an approach. It is in step, not out of step, with the march of the common law. This is the constitutional balance at work, for it integrates fundamental principle, the norms and standards that protect the individual citizen's autonomy and are the bedrock of the Rule of Law, with the legislative process. In accepting a legislative hierarchy Parliament implicitly accepts that some measures possess a higher constitutional importance, and therefore merit a higher degree of protection, than others. The legislature is thus required to treat our fundamental norms and standards, not as an alien force, but as part of its own proper function.

II. The Nature of Parliamentary Sovereignty

Despite the EU, human rights, the *dicta* in the *Jackson* case, the heresies of Parliamentary intent and *ultra vires* (as I sought to expose them in chapter 7), and the indissolubility of constitutional principle and the legislative power, the basic principle of Parliament's overriding authority has not been thrown from

---

[13] ibid 347–48.
[14] ibid 357.

its pedestal. Thus it is obvious that the courts, however great their interpretative power, cannot rewrite legislation as such: an elementary truth graphically illustrated by the divorce case of *Owens v Owens*,[15] in which the Supreme Court felt unease (to say the least) at the present state of the statutory law of divorce and called on Parliament to review the situation.

But there is a dilemma here. What if Parliament were to abridge or even overthrow our constitutional principles? I am not going to suggest that parliamentary sovereignty should simply be curtailed in a crude sense, that is by a hard-edged limitation on the power of Parliament to legislate, or the imposition of a higher power entitled to quash its legislation for inconsistency with overriding principle. That said, however, there might in theory be a statute so outrageous that any conscientious judge would think it contrary to his or her judicial oath to uphold it. Consider, for instance, clause 10 of the Asylum and Immigration (Treatment of Claimants, etc) Bill of 2003, which, had it been enacted, would have abolished any right of appeal or review to the higher courts from a negative immigration decision by the Immigration Appeal Tribunal. That would have made the Immigration Appeal Tribunal the final judge of the legality of its own decisions, disapplying *Anisminic* and overturning centuries of law that asserted the hegemony of the Queen's Bench over inferior bodies – in essence the judicial review jurisdiction. Opposition by two ex-Lord Chancellors,[16] along with many others, eventually caused the proposal to be dropped. It is interesting that in his 1994 FA Mann Lecture, Lord Woolf said there was a distinction between laws that modified the courts' powers and legislation that

> seeks to undermine in a fundamental way the Rule of Law on which our unwritten constitution depends by removing or substantially impairing the entire reviewing role of the High Court on judicial review ... I myself would consider there were advantages in making it clear that ultimately there are even limits on the supremacy of Parliament which it is the courts' inalienable responsibility to identify and uphold.[17]

The practical reality, however, is that the sharper conflicts between constitutional principle and ambitious legislation are, as I have suggested, generally overcome by the resourcefulness of statutory interpretation.[18] More broadly, we need to consider how best to categorise or describe the true nature of legislative sovereignty.

Traditional perceptions and descriptions of the sovereignty of Parliament tend to rest on the simple idea that Parliament is all-powerful. Recall Lord Neuberger's lecture, which I cited earlier in this chapter: '[e]ven the strongest advocate of limiting parliamentary authority must accept that the courts could only overrule

---

[15] *Owens v Owens* [2018] UKSC 41.

[16] Lords Mackay and Irvine.

[17] Lord Woolf 'Droit Publique: English Style', FA Mann Memorial Lecture, Lincoln's Inn (15 November 1994).

[18] Note what I said at paras 37 and 38 in *R (on the application of Cart) v Upper Tribunal* [2009] EWHC Admin 3052, [2010] 2 WLR 1012; see ch 4, section II.

parliament in wholly exceptional cases'[19] – suggesting that the touchstone of sovereignty is the (perhaps relative) immunity of statutes from being overruled. But this says nothing of the very real constraints on parliamentary power imposed by our constitutional fundamentals. These constraints, imposed by the courts through the medium, perhaps the euphemism, of statutory construction, amount to an important qualification of the very idea of parliamentary sovereignty. The legislators have to respect them. If they do not, they may find that the Act as interpreted by the courts integrates constitutional principle with the text. This recalls what I said in chapter 2, dealing with democracy: '[T]he foundational principles that give life to the Rule of Law are the very guardians of democracy's integrity. Democratic government, then, lends itself to the Rule of Law.'

The importance of the refutation of parliamentary intent (and *ultra vires*) on which I embarked in the last chapter is that it helps remove inhibitions to the process of integration, and in doing so reveals the intimacy between the power of constitutional fundamentals and the power to legislate.

Parliamentary sovereignty, then, does not rest merely on the immunity of statutes from being overruled. It is no less concerned with the practical business (and sometimes difficulty) of making law where constitutional fundamentals are integral to the process.

If we understand parliamentary sovereignty in this way we shall reduce the tension, such as it is, between political and judicial power, and at the same time serve the constitutional balance. The process is greatly assisted by the refutation of parliamentary intent and the *ultra vires* doctrine. An acceptance of legislative *purpose* (as opposed to intent) has a linked benign effect. As I said in the last chapter:

> [W]hereas the construction of a contract is an exercise devoted only to the ascertainment of its makers' intention, the interpretation of a statute involves more than the ascertainment of its purpose. The statute's construction also involves the application of our constitutional principles, which the Rule of Law imposes on the process of legislation. The problem with the idea of Parliamentary intent … is that it looks like the whole story: the only begetter of the statute's meaning. … If instead we speak of the purpose of the statute rather than the intention of the legislature, we shall avoid [this] trap; or at least we shall be less likely to fall into it.[20]

This approach, then, encapsulates what I have said in chapter 2 about democracy and in the last chapter about parliamentary intent and *ultra vires*; it means that the moralities of law and government, Kantian and utilitarian, are in harmony and not in opposition; in short it gives the Rule of Law and the constitutional balance their proper place.

---

[19] Lord Neuberger (n 4).
[20] See ch 7, section I.D.

III. Assaults on the Constitutional Balance

Without this benign alliance between power and principle, and its concrete existence in the meaning to be given to parliamentary sovereignty, the constitutional balance and our fundamental principles are particularly vulnerable to assaults, not least on the political front. David Howarth said this:

> [W]e should not be surprised to find that politicians interpret public law as essentially a political intervention by lawyers into politics and lawyers interpret it as a principled challenge to the lawlessness of politicians.[21]

I have already referred to what would have been the damaging effects of clause 10 of the Asylum and Immigration (Treatment of Claimants, etc) Bill of 2003 (section II), and to section 84 of the Criminal Justice and Courts Act 2015 (chapter 3). These two instances are, of course, concerned with legislation or legislative proposals. Assaults on the constitutional balance by the executive have tended to be rather more raw in nature. I shall give an example directly. But at this stage I would emphasise some points of principle. Political attacks, as I would characterise them, are not generally mounted out of bad faith, malice, stupidity or any other malign cause. They are usually – I would think nearly always – muscular assertions of the utilitarian morality of government; assertions made, I think it fair to say, out of a sense of entitlement induced by the democratic status of the legislature and executive conferred by the popular vote: not least given the doctrine of parliamentary sovereignty. The seduction of democratic authority can induce the political critics to forget the constitutional balance.

I shall give an example of an assault by the executive on the constitutional balance. I owe it to the same chapter of *The Cambridge Companion to Public Law*, by David Howarth. It is something of a case study. It arose out of an appeal in a case called *Izuazu*,[22] decided in the Upper Tribunal presided over by Blake J, the Tribunal President. The judgment is detailed and painstaking, and the short references I shall give cannot do the whole of it justice.

Izuazu was an appeal to the Upper Tribunal by the Secretary of State from a decision of the First-tier Tribunal, which had allowed Ms Izuazu's appeal in reliance on grounds based on Article 8 of the European Convention on Human Rights, against the Secretary of State's refusal of leave to enter the UK. Ms Izuazu had overstayed an earlier leave, and had travelled to the UK on false documents. She had been sentenced to 12 weeks' imprisonment in relation to those. On appeal to the Upper Tribunal, the Secretary of State submitted that the First-tier Tribunal had failed to consider the effect of new Immigration Rules, introduced with effect from 9 July 2012:

---

[21] D Howarth, 'The Politics of Public Law' in D Feldman and M Elliott (eds), *The Cambridge Companion to Public Law* (Cambridge University Press, 2015) ch 2, 37.

[22] *Re Izuazu (Article 8: New Rues: Nigeria)* [2013] UKUT 45.

The Secretary of State would expect the Court to defer to the view endorsed by Parliament on how, broadly, public policy considerations are weighed against individual family and private life rights, when assessing Article 8 in any individual case.[23]

The new provisions were intended, according to an accompanying Explanatory Statement, '[t]o provide a clear basis for considering immigration family and private life cases in compliance with Article 8'. Ms Isuazu did not comply with their requirements. The Secretary of State submitted that the new Rules made a substantial difference to the existing case law and restored the exceptional circumstances test disapproved by the House of Lords in *Huang v SSHD*.[24] However the Upper Tribunal concluded:

1.   In cases to which the new Immigration Rules introduced as from 9 July 2012 … apply, judges should proceed by first considering whether a claimant is able to benefit under the applicable provisions of the Immigration Rules designed to address Article 8 claims. Where the claimant does not meet the requirements of the rules it will be necessary to go on to make an assessment of Article 8 applying the criteria established by law …

2.   The procedure adopted in relation to the introduction of the new Rules provided a weak form of Parliamentary scrutiny; Parliament has not altered the legal duty of the judge determining appeals to decide on proportionality for himself or herself.

3.   There can be no presumption that the Rules will normally be conclusive of the Article 8 assessment or that a fact-sensitive inquiry is normally not needed. The more the new Rules restrict otherwise relevant and weighty considerations from being taken into account, the less regard will be had to them in the assessment of proportionality.[25]

Although the Upper Tribunal in fact *allowed* the Secretary of State's appeal, this reasoning infuriated the then Home Secretary, Mrs Theresa May. She expressed herself in strong terms in the *Mail on Sunday*:

[S]ome judges seem to believe that they can ignore Parliament's wishes if they think that the procedures for parliamentary scrutiny have been 'weak'. That appears actually to mean that they can ignore Parliament when they think it came to the wrong conclusion …

[T]he law in this country is made by the elected representatives of the people in Parliament. And our democracy is subverted when judges decide to take on that role for themselves.

And:

Just think for a moment what this judge is claiming. He is asserting that he can ignore the unanimous adoption by the Commons of new immigration rules on the grounds that he thinks this is a 'weak form of parliamentary scrutiny'.

---

[23] ibid [27].
[24] *Huang v SSHD* [2007] 2 AC 167.
[25] *Izuazu* (n 22) Headnote.

I find it difficult to see how that can be squared with the central idea of our constitution, which is that Parliament makes the law, and judges interpret what that law is and make sure the executive complies with it.[26]

Mrs May was not the first Home Secretary to excoriate the judges. As Howarth observes,[27] '[h]er Labour predecessor David Blunkett not only said that judges who refuse to accept ministers' public policy decisions constitute a "threat to democracy", but also, allegedly, called the Lord Chief Justice "a muddled and confused old codger".[28]

I do not of course suggest that the integrated view of legislative sovereignty that I have advanced will consign divisions between judges and politicians, sometimes bitter divisions, to history. There will be differences of opinion about the force of fundamental principle, and especially about where the balance lies in the individual case between the demands of principle and the demands of policy. No theory of parliamentary sovereignty can deny this reality. Apart from anything else, the pull of the contrasting moralities of law and government guarantees as much. Nor is that a bad thing. As I said in chapter 3, utilitarianism is necessarily and honourably the moral language of government. Rights and duties are necessarily and honourably the moral language of justice and therefore of law. But it is to be hoped that a revised view of sovereignty will – certainly it should – take out of the mix the destructive sense that judges and politicians are on opposite sides of the constitutional debate.

It is not only the claims of political power that can upset the constitutional balance. The courts can do it too. They are sometimes vulnerable to pressures arising from the law of human rights that encourage them in that direction. I shall deal with human rights more fully in the next chapter. But it will be recalled that in chapter 3 I referred to the deportation of foreign criminals: should the clear statutory policy of removing such a criminal from the UK prevail over the criminal's claim under Article 8 of the Convention to enjoy family life with his or her children born in this jurisdiction? There is a danger, sometimes turned into reality, that in some cases the grant of Article 8 rights may unjustifiably outweigh the proper claims of public interest.

IV. *Auctoritas* and *Imperium*

That brings me, at the end, to introduce a little ancient history. If the comparison is not pressed too far, the distinction recognised in ancient Rome during both the republican and the imperial eras between two forms of power, *auctoritas* and

---

[26] I take these quotations from Howarth (n 21) 38 and 39.

[27] ibid 39.

[28] For this ' allegation' Howarth cites R Stevens, *The English Judges: Their Role in the Changing Constitution* (Hart Publishing, 2005) 173.

imperium, may I think tell us something of the route by which the strict doctrine of legislative sovereignty may be qualified or moderated consistently with public tranquility and the proper claims of democratic rule. Very broadly, *imperium* meant power conferred by law, the formal power of rule or command, especially over the military: it was possessed by the consuls and praetors and other senior magistrates. *Auctoritas* was more elusive, or seems so to modern eyes. It had over-tones of reputation and of moral authority. It is associated in particular with the Emperor Augustus, who established the Principate after the Battle of Actium in 31 BC. What was called the *auctoritas principis* described his personal authority, the quality that allowed him to gather and to keep the dignified powers of the republican magistrates, and to settle the new imperial regime.

Obviously I intend no direct comparison between the constitutional position of the UK Parliament and the concepts of power that prevailed in ancient Rome. My point is only that the idea of sovereignty need not reside, and in the UK does not reside, only in the formality of hard legal power. If the State is to be tranquil, the legislature, especially if it aspires to sovereignty, must possess something akin to *auctoritas* as well as out-and-out *imperium*. Because Parliament's legislation is not limited to cold command but may range across the kaleidoscope of human welfare, secure in the moderating influence of the law's foundational principles, its authority – its *auctoritas* – is enhanced. It may obtain the trust, and not merely the subservience, of the people. Sovereignty is by no means only a matter of *imperium*. But it requires a self-limiting ordinance: respect for constitutional principle. Such an ordinance, which is not far distant from the idea of *auctoritas*, may be seen as a condition of sovereignty.

It may be said that the recognition of moral authority – *auctoritas* – as a feature of our constitutional arrangements broadens the scope of our enquiry from law pure and simple into the field of sociology, or something very like it. Are we concerned with the wisdom or acumen of our legislators, as well as with their objective legal powers? Immanuel Kant said this: 'We must not expect a good constitution because those who make it are moral men. Rather it is because of a good constitution that we may expect a society composed of moral men.'[29]

Such an antithesis raises speculative questions well beyond the reach of this chapter. I am concerned only to demonstrate that the sovereignty of Parliament demands *auctoritas* as well as *imperium*: it rules, or should rule, with the will of the people; but that means more than the quinquennial visit to the ballot-box. It requires that hard power be tempered by constitutional principle: as I would put it, by our foundational principles of reason, fairness and the presumption of liberty. But constitutional principle is undermined if the supposed intention of Parliament is set on the throne of statutory interpretation.

---

[29] Quoted by L Fuller, *The Morality of Law* (Yale University Press, rev edn 1969) 152.

9

Human Rights, Free Thought and Expression

I. Human Rights

With the exception of certain parts of sections 12[1] and 13,[2] which seem to me to add little more than rhetoric, the Human Rights Act 1998 (HRA 1998) is an elegant, well-drafted statute.

The Act of 1998, which of course incorporated the European Convention on Human Rights (ECHR) into British law, may be seen as an important facilitator of the constitutional balance, or conversely as a primrose path leading the judges (or some of them) to upset the balance. Both possibilities arise from the qualified rights given by Articles 8–11 of the Convention:

ARTICLE 8

Right to respect for private and family life

1. Everyone has the right to respect for his private and family life, his home and his correspondence.
2. There shall be no interference by a public authority with the exercise of this right except such as is in accordance with the law and is necessary in a democratic society in the interests of national security, public safety or the economic well-being of the country, for the prevention of disorder or crime, for the protection of health or morals, or for the protection of the rights and freedoms of others.

ARTICLE 9

Freedom of thought, conscience and religion

1. Everyone has the right to freedom of thought, conscience and religion; this right includes freedom to change his religion or belief and freedom, either alone or in community with others and in public or private, to manifest his religion or belief, in worship, teaching, practice and observance.

---

[1] HRA 1998, s 12(4): 'The court must have particular regard to the importance of the Convention right to freedom of expression …'.
[2] HRA 1998, s 13(1): 'If a court's determination of any question arising under this Act might affect the exercise by a religious organisation … of the Convention right to freedom of thought, conscience and religion, it must have particular regard to the importance of that right.'

2.   Freedom to manifest one's religion or beliefs shall be subject only to such limitations as are prescribed by law and are necessary in a democratic society in the interests of public safety, for the protection of public order, health or morals, or for the protection of the rights and freedoms of others.

ARTICLE 10

Freedom of expression

1.   Everyone has the right to freedom of expression. This right shall include freedom to hold opinions and to receive and impart information and ideas without interference by public authority and regardless of frontiers. This Article shall not prevent States from requiring the licensing of broadcasting, television or cinema enterprises.
2.   The exercise of these freedoms, since it carries with it duties and responsibilities, may be subject to such formalities, conditions, restrictions or penalties as are prescribed by law and are necessary in a democratic society, in the interests of national security, territorial integrity or public safety, for the prevention of disorder or crime, for the protection of health or morals, for the protection of the reputation or rights of others, for preventing the disclosure of information received in confidence, or for maintaining the authority and impartiality of the judiciary.

ARTICLE 11

Freedom of assembly and association

1.   Everyone has the right to freedom of peaceful assembly and to freedom of association with others, including the right to form and join trade unions for the protection of his interests.
2.   No restrictions shall be placed on the exercise of these rights other than such as are prescribed by law and are necessary in a democratic society in the interests of national security or public safety, for the prevention of disorder or crime, for the protection of health or morals or for the protection of the rights and freedoms of others. This Article shall not prevent the imposition of lawful restrictions on the exercise of these rights by members of the armed forces, of the police or of the administration of the State.

It will be seen at once that these Articles invoke a balance between the conferment of the right and the power of the State to abrogate or diminish the right in the name of the public interest. This should be a recipe or template for the practical fulfilment of the constitutional balance, and when the system works properly that is what it is. But there are a number of difficulties in its path.

A. Problems for the Constitutional Balance: The ECHR and the Strasbourg Jurisprudence

In none of Articles 8–11 is there any provision that indicates the function of decision-making between government and courts respectively. It is perhaps unsurprising that the drafters of the ECHR were not greatly concerned with which arm of the State – legislature, executive or judiciary – was or was not in compliance with the Convention duties: whichever it was, the European Court of Human Rights ('the Strasbourg Court') was there to require compliance. As Professor Feldman has said, '[the court] decides where a *State*, not an institution within a State, has violated a person's Convention right'.[3] This means, however, that there is nothing on the face of the ECHR to recognise the impact of the domestic constitutional balance. It goes without saying that other States may see the constitutional balance differently, though if it goes unrecognised in any polity – if the two moralities are not in constellation with each other – there are dangers. As I said in chapter 3, 'The constitutional balance requires that the two moralities are so far as possible in harmony; each of them served to the least prejudice of the other.'

The Strasbourg Court has developed the well-known doctrine of the margin of appreciation to allow for a degree of discretionary space in the hands of national authorities in their approach to the Convention obligations. The doctrine has its origin in Civilian jurisprudence, not least that of the French *Conseil d'Etat*. It is reflected in the passage from Lord Hope's speech in *Kebilene*.[4] But the focus of the doctrine is not intended to cater for variations between the decision-making roles of government and courts within the signatory States. Rather it is distinctly the creature of an international tribunal, providing some scope to the individual States to decide for themselves (by whatever means) whether a substantive violation of a Convention right has been perpetrated, subject always to the Strasbourg Court's ultimate power of judgment. It seems, then, that the Convention has nothing to tell us about the way in which the courts should view their decision-making role in human rights cases.

The jurisprudence of the Strasbourg Court is obviously not concerned with the specifics of the British constitution. As I have said, its doctrine of the margin of appreciation is fashioned to provide a degree of discretionary space to the national authorities to decide on particular facts whether there has been a violation of Convention rights. The court has held that a wide margin of appreciation may be accorded to the States where, for example, 'having regard to the diversity of the practices followed and the situations obtaining in the Contracting States, the ... requirements [ie of the Convention right in question] will vary considerably from case to case'.[5] But plainly such an approach draws no distinction between the respective roles of courts and government within the signatory States.

In that particular case (which was concerned with Article 8) the Court continued:

> In particular, in the area now under consideration, the extent of a State's obligation to admit to its territory relatives of settled immigrants will vary according to the particular circumstances of the persons involved.[6]

---

[3] D Feldman, *Sovereignty and the Law* (Oxford University Press, 2013) ch 12, 224.
[4] *R v DPP, ex parte Kebilene* [2000] 2 AC 326.
[5] *Abdulaziz, Cabales and Balkandali v United Kingdom* (1985) 7 EHRR 471, para 67.
[6] ibid.

This observation illustrates, I think (as does the Court's subsequent careful examination of the circumstances of the particular applicants), the fact-specific character of many of the Strasbourg Court's judgments: a quality that hardly betrays a concern that domestic courts should restrain themselves and allow a broad area of discretion to their municipal governments. This fact-specific quality is also illustrated by the case of *Uner*,[7] in which the Court set out in detail and at length the factual criteria it would apply in deciding whether the expulsion of a foreign criminal was justified under Article 8(2) ECHR.

B. The Human Rights Act

I should set out the following provisions of the HRA 1998.

2. Interpretation of Convention rights

(1)   A court or tribunal determining a question which has arisen in connection with a Convention right must take into account any—

(a)   judgment, decision, declaration or advisory opinion of the European Court of Human Rights,

…

whenever made or given, so far as, in the opinion of the court or tribunal, it is relevant to the proceedings in which that question has arisen.

3. Interpretation of legislation

(1)   So far as it is possible to do so, primary legislation and subordinate legislation must be read and given effect in a way which is compatible with the Convention rights.

…

4. Declaration of incompatibility

(1)   Subsection (2) applies in any proceedings in which a court determines whether a provision of primary legislation is compatible with a Convention right.

(2)   If the court is satisfied that the provision is incompatible with a Convention right, it may make a declaration of that incompatibility.

…

6. Acts of public authorities

(1)   It is unlawful for a public authority to act in a way which is incompatible with a Convention right.

(2)   Subsection (1) does not apply to an act if—

(a)   as the result of one or more provisions of primary legislation, the authority could not have acted differently …

…

---

[7] *Uner v The Netherlands* (2007) 45 EHRR 14, paras 57–58.

(3)   In this section 'public authority' includes—

   (a)   a court or tribunal, and

   (b)   any person certain of whose functions are functions of a public nature,

but does not include either House of Parliament or a person exercising functions in connection with proceedings in Parliament.

...

Section 7 entitles a person claiming that a public authority has acted contrary to section 6 to bring proceedings (though if the authority is a court, in accordance with section 9, only by way of appeal or judicial review).

The HRA 1998, though careful to preserve the sovereignty of Parliament (see section 4(2)), says no more than the Strasbourg Court about the degree of judicial deference owed to the elected arms of government in deciding the strength in any given case of a public interest defence raised by government under paragraph (2) of any of Articles 8–11. As I have said, the constitutional balance seems to play no part, overtly at least, in the human rights scheme of things.

C. Consequences

The courts have had to develop some kind of pattern by which private right may be balanced against public interest. In the *Roth* case,[8] cited in chapter 6, I sought to develop four principles as a broad basis on which to distribute the relative force to be accorded to these often competing interests. They did not, of course, purport to constitute any kind of code or rule. Nor could they; nor could the legislature. The balance to be struck between public and private interest is not amenable to codes or rules. It requires judgement, sometimes nuanced judgement.

As I have indicated, many of the Strasbourg Court's judgments are highly fact-specific. A consequence of the *Ullah* mistake (see section I.D) was that our courts and tribunals have to some extent felt driven to align their decisions as to whether or not there was a breach of a Convention right with the conclusions of the Strasbourg Court in what were (or seemed to be) similar instances. In *SS (Nigeria)*,[9] to which I referred in chapters 5 and 6, the Upper Tribunal (though it allowed the Secretary of State's appeal from the First-tier Tribunal 'on balance') cited the whole of the Strasbourg Court's summary in *Uner*[10] of the matters to be considered in deciding whether an expulsion measure was justified.

Our tribunals' relative loyalty to the Strasbourg Court's merits-based approach tended to marginalise any deference due from the courts to the elected powers as

---

[8] *International Transport Roth GmbH v Secretary of State for the Home Department* [2003] QB 728, paras 83–85, 87.

[9] *SS (Nigeria) v Secretary of State for the Home Department* [2014] 1 WLR 998.

[10] *Uner v The Netherlands* [2006] ECHR 873.

regards the merits of individual cases. Instead of developing a domestic approach to the Convention rights, which would have paid full regard not only to local conditions but also to the imperative of the constitutional balance, we were inclined to confine the law in a Strasbourg straitjacket.

As a result, it seemed to many that the judges had too big a say on issues raising questions of policy and public interest (the foreign criminal case was a conspicuous example) – and not just any judges, but the Strasbourg judges at that. No doubt some of the criticism was overblown, fuelled more by prejudice than rational thought. There are always going to be people who dislike the notion of rights enjoyed by the unmeritorious, and I suppose we shall never be entirely free of the odour of xenophobia. But there was a real point, or rather two points: the law of human rights was to a considerable extent being administered with insufficient regard for the constitutional balance, and the autonomous development of human rights law by the common law courts was undermined.

The importance of the lack of any steer in the ECHR or the Act towards the constitutional balance is not the want of any rules; it is rather that decision-makers may simply go about their task as if the constitutional balance played no part in it, or at least no critical part. One result is that a unified understanding of the sovereignty of Parliament, in which constitutional principle and State policy are integrated, is all the more difficult to achieve.

There will always be differences of opinion between courts and government over issues concerning the balance to be struck between private right and public interest. The case of the foreign criminal who claims to remain in the UK by force of Article 8 ECHR is, as I have said, a good example. A recognition of the constitutional balance will not obliterate such differences, but it should foster an understanding that courts and government are not on opposite side of an unbridgeable gap but are bringing different perspectives to a single aspiration: democracy informed and tempered by constitutional principle. The HRA 1998 and the Convention should foster this aspiration, not undermine it.

D. The *Ullah* Case

There is, however, another problem, though it seems to be on the wane. Its origin lies in a passage in Lord Bingham's speech in *Ullah v Special Adjudicator*,[11] in which judgment was given in June 2004. Lord Bingham said this:

> [T]he House is required by section 2(1) of the Human Rights Act 1998 to take into account any relevant Strasbourg case law. While such case law is not strictly binding, it has been held that courts should, in the absence of some special circumstances, follow any clear and constant jurisprudence of the Strasbourg court: *R (Alconbury Developments*

---

[11] *Ullah v Special Adjudicator* [2004] 2 AC 323.

Ltd) v Secretary of State for the Environment, Transport and the Regions [2001] UKHL 23, [2003] 2 AC 295, paragraph 26. This reflects the fact that the Convention is an international instrument, the correct interpretation of which can be authoritatively expounded only by the Strasbourg court. From this it follows that a national court subject to a duty such as that imposed by section 2 should not without strong reason dilute or weaken the effect of the Strasbourg case law. It is indeed unlawful under section 6 of the 1998 Act for a public authority, including a court, to act in a way which is incompatible with a Convention right. It is of course open to member states to provide for rights more generous than those guaranteed by the Convention, but such provision should not be the product of interpretation of the Convention by national courts, since the meaning of the Convention should be uniform throughout the states party to it. The duty of national courts is to keep pace with the Strasbourg jurisprudence as it evolves over time: no more, but certainly no less.[12]

The vice of this passage, not least the last sentence, is that it seems to confer authority on the Strasbourg Court to steer or even decide issues touching the constitutional balance that are properly within the domain of the United Kingdom (UK) courts, and which should firmly remain there. Section 2 of the HRA 1998 does not justify such a state of affairs, with which, in fact, it is inconsistent. Moreover, the first two sentences seem to me to contain a *non sequitur*. Given the language of section 2 ('take into account'), the fact that the Strasbourg Court is the authoritative source of the ECHR's interpretation does not entail the proposition 'that a national court subject to a duty such as that imposed by section 2 should not without strong reason dilute or weaken the effect of the Strasbourg case law'.

Closely allied to *Ullah* is a passage from Lord Sumption's judgment in *Chester*:

[A] decision of the European Court of Human Rights … is an adjudication by the tribunal which the United Kingdom has by treaty agreed should give definitive rulings on the subject. The courts are therefore bound to treat them as the authoritative expositions of the Convention …[13]

Thus the House of Lords and the Supreme Court have accorded overriding force to the notion that only Strasbourg's rulings on the Convention are 'definitive' or 'authoritative'. The argument must be that unless our courts follow the Strasbourg jurisprudence, they will violate their duty, under section 6 of the 1998 Act, to act compatibly with the Convention rights. But this proposition, and the vice of *Ullah* that I have briefly described, involves two mistakes. The first is that it ignores, or at least distorts, the effect of section 2 of the HRA 1998. The duty there prescribed is to 'take into account' the jurisprudence of the Strasbourg Court. As Lord Sumption said in *Chester*, '[i]n the ordinary use of language, to "take into account" a decision of the European Court of Human Rights means no more than to consider it, which is consistent with rejecting it as wrong'.[14] The statutory

---

[12] ibid para 20. Cf Lord Brown in *Al-Skeini* [2007] UKHL 26.
[13] *R (Chester) v Secretary of State for Justice* [2013] UKSC 63, [2014] AC 271, [121].
[14] ibid.

purpose, taking sections 2 and 6 together, must in my view be that the section 6 duty is to be applied and understood by reference to our domestic courts' own appreciation of the Convention rights, taking into account, but not necessarily following, the Strasbourg jurisprudence; however, as I have said, such an autonomous development of human rights law by the common law courts was undermined by the *Ullah* approach.

But I think there is a second, perhaps deeper, mistake in the *Ullah* line of reasoning. The notion of 'the correct interpretation' of the Convention (*Ullah*) or the Strasbourg Court's 'definitive rulings' (*Chester*) is not as straightforward as it seems. That is so, first, because (as I have said) the Court's rulings tend to be fact-sensitive – and a judgment that does no more than apply established principle to individual facts is generally no precedent for future cases; and, second, because the idea of a single authoritative interpretation of the Convention diminishes the Court's own doctrine of the margin of appreciation. It fails to pay sufficient heed to the fact that, as the Strasbourg Court has itself said, 'having regard to the diversity of the practices followed and the situations obtaining in the Contracting States, the ... requirements [ie of the Convention right in question] will vary considerably from case to case'.[15] The UK is of course bound to fulfil decisions of the Strasbourg Court in cases to which it is itself a party; but the *Ullah* line of reasoning draws no distinction between that and other cases to which the UK is a complete stranger. It may of course rightly be said that there is a difference between a principle and its application. But the practical deployment of Articles 8–11 ECHR (apart from the interpretation, in many cases, of the term 'necessary in a democratic society', which appears in each of the Articles, to mean 'proportionate) is effectively all application.

There would be no denial of the Convention rights in a decision of our courts that respects the constitutional balance, and which therefore gives a degree – perhaps a decisive degree – of deference to the elected powers' view of the public interest.

E. *Ullah* in Retreat

Ullah has been very influential. There have, however, been eloquent calls for looser ties between our courts and Strasbourg for some time. Lord Irvine of Lairg and Jack Straw MP, who sponsored the Human Rights Bill in the Lords and Commons respectively, have been muscular advocates for such an outcome: Jack Straw in the second of his Hamlyn Lectures delivered in 2012.[16] So has Baroness Hale,

---

[15] *Abdulaziz, Cabales and Balkandali* (n 5).

[16] J Straw, *Aspects of Law Reform: an Insider's Perspective* (Hamlyn Lectures, 2012) ch 2, 'The Human Rights Act and Europe'. Lord Irvine gave a lecture entitled *A British Interpretation of Convention Rights* at the UCL Judicial Institute on 14 December 2011. Sir Philip Sales published a reply, 'Strasbourg Jurisprudence and the Human Rights Act: A Response to Lord Irvine' [2012] *PL* 253.

speaking extra-judicially.[17] And Lord Reed, in a lecture at the Inner Temple in 2013,[18] expounded and emphasised the primacy of the common law's protection of human rights.

The reality is that there has been an increasing degree of slippage from the unqualified *Ullah* position. Lord Phillips, in a 2010 case,[19] referred to

> rare occasions where the domestic court has concerns as to whether a decision of the Strasbourg court sufficiently appreciates or accommodates particular aspects of our domestic process. In such circumstances it is open to the domestic court to decline to follow the Strasbourg decision, giving reasons for adopting this course.[20]

More positively, Lord Neuberger has stated that

> [t]his court is not bound to follow every decision of the European court. Not only would it be impractical to do so: it would sometimes be inappropriate, as it would destroy the ability of the court to engage in the constructive dialogue with the European court which is of value to the development of Convention law.[21]

Still more recently, our courts have become readier to spread their wings. In *AG's Reference No 69 of 2013*,[22] in which judgment was delivered on 18 February 2014, the Criminal Division of the Court of Appeal had to address the reasoning of the Grand Chamber of the European Court of Human Rights in *Vinter*,[23] which concerned provisions of UK law relevant to the imposition of whole-life prison terms. The Strasbourg Court had regard to the Secretary of State's power under section 30 of the Crime (Sentences) Act 1997, to 'release a life prisoner on licence if he is satisfied that exceptional circumstances exist which justify the prisoner's release on compassionate grounds'. In the *AG's Reference* case, the Lord Chief Justice summarised the Strasbourg Court's reasoning:

> The Grand Chamber therefore concluded that s 30 did not, because of the lack of certainty, provide an appropriate and adequate avenue of redress in the event an offender sought to show that his continued imprisonment was not justified.[24]

Paragraph 129 of the Strasbourg judgment is then cited, setting out the Court's reasoning. The Lord Chief Justice concluded:

> We disagree. In our view, the domestic law of England and Wales is clear as to 'possible exceptional release of whole life prisoners'.[25]

---

[17] B Hale, *Argentoratum Locutum: Is the Supreme Court Supreme?* (Nottingham Human Rights Lecture 2011, 1 December 2011).
[18] Lord Reed, *The Common Law and the ECHR* (Inner Temple, 11 November 2013).
[19] *R v Horncastle* [2010] 2 AC 373.
[20] ibid para 11.
[21] *Manchester City Council v Pinnock* [2011] 2 AC 104, para 48.
[22] *AG's Reference No 69 of 2013, R v McLoughlin* [2014] EWCA Crim 188, [2014] 1 WLR 3964.
[23] *Vinter v the United Kingdom* App Nos 66069/09, 130/10 and 3896/10 [2013] ECHR 645; (2016) 63 EHRR 1.
[24] *AG's Reference No 69 of 2013* (n 22) [28].
[25] ibid [29].

In *Hutchinson*,[26] another whole-life sentence case from the UK in which the judgment of the Grand Chamber was delivered on 17 January 2017, the Strasbourg Court set out substantial extracts from the Court of Appeal's judgment in the *AG's Reference* case and concluded that 'the Court of Appeal has brought clarity as to the content of the relevant domestic law'.[27] After considering other Strasbourg cases decided since *Vinter*, the Court held that 'the whole life sentence can now be regarded as reducible, in keeping with Article 3 of the Convention'.[28]

The majority judgment of the Grand Chamber in the *Hutchinson* case is a good example of the 'constructive dialogue' between London and Strasbourg to which Lord Neuberger referred. I should note, perhaps by way of contrast, that the dissenting judgment of Judge Pinto de Albuquerque contains a fascinating critique of the evolving treatment of section 2 of the HRA 1998.

Generally, it may I suppose be thought that the *Ullah* debate is by now getting a little long in the tooth; but it is important to understand it if we are to get to grips with the imperatives of the constitutional balance, and therefore with the protection of the Rule of Law.

II. Free Thought and Expression

It may be thought that these ideas hardly need separate treatment: they are integral to our three constitutional principles, not least the presumption of liberty. But they require special emphasis, for they are a critical premise on which those very principles, and the constitutional balance, depend. Moreover, free expression is under attack, and I should confront that.

Consider again the essential elements of the presumption of liberty, which I discussed in chapter 5: (i) for the individual citizen, everything that is not forbidden is allowed; (ii) for public bodies, and notably government, everything that is not allowed is forbidden; (iii) every intrusion by the State upon the freedom of the individual stands in need of objective justification (the principle of minimal interference). Each of these propositions proceeds on the premise that under the good constitution the individual citizen is free to think and do as he or she chooses. As regards his or her actions (but not his or her thoughts), that is subject only to considerations relating to such overriding interests as national security, the prevention of crime and the rights of others (see Article 10(2) ECHR): in particular, such constraints as are needed to ensure that every other citizen enjoys the same autonomy. This is the principle that links the ideal of a just society of free people with the imperative of the Rule of Law. Our three propositions, the essential

---

[26] *Hutchinson v United Kingdom* App no 57592/08 (ECtHR, 17 January 2017).
[27] ibid para 40; cf para 70.
[28] ibid para 72.

elements of the presumption of liberty, both require the validation of free thought and action, and take their place as the constitutional framework that makes it happen. They make the constitutional balance both possible and necessary.

Free thought, which is a condition of every person's flourishing, needs free expression; free expression, therefore, is a condition of the presumption of liberty and therefore of the Rule of Law. The central idea of human freedom is surely the idea of choice, and the maximisation of choice; and that means informed choice. To the extent that a person lacks this power of choice – lacks autonomy – his or decisions (so far as he or she makes any) are adrift, rootless, unprincipled. They are likely to be dictated to him or her by fear or lust, by unthinking assumptions, or by a real or imagined external source, man or god, whose utterance he or she treats as holy writ, incontrovertible law, to be obeyed without question, perhaps on pain of unspeakable punishments. I said in the Introduction that the bare existence of a master's command is of itself no basis whatever to require the servant's obedience. It is an instance of Hume's Law: you cannot derive an *ought* from an *is*.

The man without autonomy is profoundly unfree. He does not choose what religion he will practise, what politics he will follow. In effect they are dictated to him; at any rate, he accepts them blindly. He is, so to speak, a billiard ball rather than a cue. But choice is not choice at all unless it is informed and rational choice; informed and rational choice is impossible, or at least hopelessly diminished, without the free exchange of ideas; and the free exchange of ideas of course requires the institution of free expression.

Free speech, then, is a necessary condition of difference and disputation; of pluralism. And, as I said in chapter 2, the imperative of pluralism – the prevention of tyranny – is the best justification for democratic rule: democracy tends to disable would-be tyrants, intent on suppressing dissent. And (see again chapter 2) our foundational principles – reason, fairness and the presumption of liberty – are the constitution's prophylactic against arbitrary, capricious law; and therefore, because they confine democracy, they are the very guardians of democracy's integrity. The flourishing of free speech, then, is a condition alike of pluralism, of democracy, of our foundational principles and of the constitutional balance. Its importance for our democracy is underlined by Article 9 of the Bill of Rights 1689: 'the freedom of speech and debates or proceedings in Parliament ought not to be impeached or questioned in any court or place out of Parliament'. And it is little surprise that by section 12(4) of the HRA 1998 (though I have criticised the provision), courts are enjoined to 'have particular regard to the importance of the Convention right to freedom of expression'.

A. Free Expression under Attack

Free expression is on the defensive today. Not so much from overt legal measures curbing free speech, though I shall come to that directly. The worrying assaults are more subtle. They grow out of an increasingly fashionable intolerance of unpopular opinion; a cowardly response to the barbarous views and practices sanctioned in some sections of society; and the gloss of political correctness. It is ironic that much of the fault may be laid at the door of liberal instincts, which, among other things, sometimes betray a reluctance to confront and condemn extremism as it should be condemned. All of this, I acknowledge, occupies a much broader canvas than the reach of this book. But it touches the law at various points, and the law – the Rule of Law – must give no quarter to the enemies of free speech. Its enemies are not all straightforward. Some of them lurk in unexpected places. Some are hard to get to grips with. But the Rule of Law has to live in the practical world, and the practical world has rough edges.

I shall start with the more obvious kind of assault on free speech: its outright prohibition. We must revisit the *ProLife* case,[29] to which I referred in chapter 6 in discussing judicial deference.

ProLife Alliance – ProLife – was a political party that, as Lord Nicholls was to say in the House of Lords, campaigned for 'absolute respect for innocent human life from fertilisation until natural death'. Among its principal policies was the prohibition of abortion. In May 2001, ProLife fielded enough candidates for the June 2001 general election to entitle it make one party election broadcast in Wales. Lord Nicholls continued:

> Early in May 2001 ProLife Alliance submitted a tape of its proposed broadcast to BBC, ITV, Channel 4 and Channel 5. The major part of the proposed programme was devoted to explaining the processes involved in different forms of abortion, with prolonged and graphic images of the product of suction abortion: aborted foetuses in a mangled and mutilated state, tiny limbs, a separated head, and the like. Unquestionably the pictures are deeply disturbing. Unquestionably many people would find them distressing, even harrowing. Representatives of each broadcaster refused to screen these pictures as part of the proposed broadcast.[30]

The broadcasters' refusals were based on their obligation (under the BBC Agreement and, in the case of the independent channels, the Broadcasting Act 1990) to secure that 'nothing is included in [their] programmes which offends against good taste or decency or is likely … to be offensive to public feeling'. ProLife brought judicial review proceedings. They were dismissed at first instance. The Court of Appeal allowed ProLife's appeal. I said:

> 36. [A]s a matter of domestic law the courts owe a special responsibility to the public as the constitutional guardian of the freedom of political debate. This responsibility is most acute at the time and in the context of a public election, especially a general election. It has its origin in a deeper truth, which is that the courts are ultimately the trustees of our democracy's framework. I consider that this view is consonant with the common law's general recognition, apparent in recent years, of a category of fundamental or constitutional rights …
>
> …

---

[29] *ProLife Alliance v BBC* [2002] EWCA Civ 297, [2004] AC 185.
[30] ibid [3].

44. There may be instances, even in the context of a general election, in which political speech may justifiably be censored on grounds of taste or offensiveness. But in my judgment it would take a very extreme case, most likely involving factors ... such as gratuitous sensationalism and dishonesty ... On the facts of this case the broadcasters have in my judgment failed altogether to give sufficient weight to the pressing imperative of free political expression. ...

By a majority of 4:1 the House of Lords took a different view. The House held, in effect, that the broadcasters had properly applied the taste and decency provisions of the BBC Agreement and the Broadcasting Act. Professor Trevor Allan criticises this approach. He opines that the Lords' decision

> effectively reduces the legal or constitutional order to the content of the discrete instructions contained in specific legislation, with minimal attention to the broader political context ... If freedom of speech is a genuine value, generating a constitutional right to free expression of political opinion, it must colour and inform an interpretative reconstruction of what, in the particular circumstances, a statutory text should be understood to mean.[31]

It will come as no surprise that I think these criticisms are well-founded. But the importance of *ProLife* for present purposes is what it has to teach about the constitutional balance. As I said in chapter 6, deference and the creative use of statutory interpretation condition the courts' duty in any given case to find the edge or limit of statutory public power: judicial deference pulls in favour of democratic government and the utilitarian morality of government; creative statutory interpretation pulls in favour of constitutional principle and the Kantian morality of the common law. *ProLife*, of course, was not concerned with governmental statutory power as such, but with the duty of broadcasters to regulate what might be broadcast to the public. However, the applicable taste and decency provisions, though expressed as a duty, in practical terms contained a power to prohibit the broadcast of certain material. There was no suggestion that the judicial review jurisdiction was not apt to supervise the power's exercise. So the courts were required, just as surely as in the case of any exercise of governmental discretion, to decide whether the decisions of the BBC and the independent channels to ban ProLife's broadcast overstepped their proper limit. Deference and creative statutory interpretation were both in play: the Lords' judgment deferred to the broadcasters, and so pulled in favour of the power's democratic source; the Court of Appeal's judgment interpreted the power in light of the free speech imperative, and so pulled in favour of constitutional principle.

If, as I have suggested, the flourishing of free speech is a condition alike of pluralism, democracy, the constitutional balance and the foundational principles, it was the Court of Appeal that pulled in the right direction. The House of Lords failed to recognise the force of the constitutional imperative behind the judicial

---

[31] TRS Allan, *The Sovereignty of Law* (Oxford University Press, 2013) 27.

review challenge. They marked the edge or limit of the broadcasters' function of censorship in the wrong place.

B. Offensive Speech

A person who is guilty of offensive speech about another's beliefs is surely entitled to exactly the same rights as the believer: including the right to think that the other's beliefs are an abomination, and the right to say so. In the realm of free speech, no one is master. Subject to legal constraints such as the law of defamation, no one has a bigger right of free expression because what he or she has to say is truer or wiser than what the next person has to say. For this reason the value of free expression implies a harder truth. It is that this value, free expression, is in a well-ordered State morally prior to the content of any person's belief. That is to say: the supposed truth of a belief never justifies the suppression of its critics' voices, and the supposed falsity of a belief never justifies suppression of the voices of its supporters. Free expression means that critics and supporters meet on equal terms. Any other view ultimately implies a dictatorship of ideas, and a dictatorship of ideas implies a dictatorship at large.

It is therefore little surprise that there are very many *dicta*, from our own courts and from the European Court of Human Rights at Strasbourg, that emphasise the central importance of free speech. I shall give just one example from Strasbourg. In *Observer and Guardian v UK*[32] (the 'Spycatcher' case), the Court of Human Rights stated:

> Freedom of expression constitutes one of the essential foundations of a democratic society; subject to paragraph (2) of Article 10, it is applicable not only to 'information' or 'ideas' that are favourably received or regarded as inoffensive or as a matter of indifference, but also to those that offend, shock or disturb. Freedom of expression, as enshrined in Article 10, is subject to a number of exceptions which, however, must be narrowly interpreted and the necessity for any restrictions must be convincingly established.[33]

This important principle is as I have said under attack. It is under attack in some of our universities, where so-called 'safe spaces' deny a platform to unpopular opinions. On a wider canvas, Dame Louise Casey's *Review into Opportunity and Integration*, describes instances in which persons with public responsibilities have failed to speak out against harmful practices out of fear or cowardice:

> 11.8. There are numerous examples which were brought to our attention during the review of local authorities, agencies and individuals bending over backwards to 'accommodate' people from minority faiths or 'different' cultures ...

---

[32] *Observer and Guardian v UK* (1992) 14 EHRR 153.
[33] ibid, para 59 of the majority judgment.

11.9. Perhaps more worryingly, among local political leadership, it might be that diffi-cult issues are ignored because political leaders are focussing on what they think their communities want to hear, rather than what they believe is right, for fear of losing the support of a particular community. That is an approach that lacks the courage and integrity people want from their representatives and which are reflected in the Nolan principles of public life; and in the worst cases can cause significant harm.[34]

My purpose is not, of course, to express any view about the substantive social problems addressed by Dame Louise Casey, but only to underline the dangers – the constitutional dangers – that face us if free expression is severely shaken. I say the dangers are constitutional because the diminution of free speech begets a censorship of ideas. Such a process would necessarily undermine, in the long term and perhaps sooner than we might think, the security of foundational princi-ples of reason, fairness and the presumption of liberty. They can only develop and thrive through the free exchange of ideas. The danger is not to be dismissed merely because the censorship is not promoted by the State.

An attack on free speech, then, is in the end an attack on the Rule of Law itself. The wheel turns full circle: we saw in chapter 1 that the foundational principles, which are integral to the Rule of Law, are woven into the law by the process of independent adjudication, in large measure by the operation of the judicial review jurisdiction; and the judicial review jurisdiction has effect through the fourfold methodology of the common law, which I described in chapter 4. We can see now that this process, which is at the core of our constitution, is eroded by the erosion of free expression.

C. Religion

I had something to say about religion in the Introduction, addressing the vice of the command theory of morals. But it has an important to play in the context of assaults on free expression. In particular a reluctance, sometimes a vehement reluctance, to give offence to the beliefs of other persons seems to arise with partic-ular frequency in the sphere of religion.

There is surely no good reason why a religious belief should be specially protected, or specially condemned, by comparison with, say, a political belief. Roughly speaking, there seems to be a good deal of consensus – notwithstanding the *ProLife* decision in the House of Lords – to the effect that assaults on political speech, however vigorous – however offensive – should not be stifled save in very special circumstances, where it may encourage or give rise to criminal activity or is injurious to national security or otherwise threatens a well-established objective value, and the threat can be tested by evidence. As regards politics, then, a society

---

[34] Dame Louise Casey DBE CB, *Casey Review: a review into opportunity and integration* (December 2016), available at https://assets.publishing.service.gov.uk/government/uploads/system/uploads/attachment_data/file/575973/The_Casey_Review_Report.pdf.

that is free and democratic has in general little difficulty applying the rule that in the realm of free speech there are no masters. Political ideas may be expressed, and assaulted, in equal measure. Critics and supporters meet on equal terms. So long as political opinion rests on reason and evidence, it can co-exist with this rule perfectly comfortably. The tenets of anyone's politics are always, so to speak, up for grabs. Its lifeblood is argument. It is honed on the anvil of disagreement. You cannot blaspheme against it. It may even relish being ridiculed, and turn the ridicule in its favour: knowing there is no worse advocacy than putting your case too high.

But when it comes to religion, liberal opinion has rather lost its way. It is sometimes much less comfortable with the idea that religious opinions are, or should be, as open to vigorous debate and disagreement as political ideas. Religion is not like politics. Its truth is held by its adherents to be sacred, inviolable. To some believers, if their faith is assaulted, certainly if it is ridiculed, that is blasphemy, or at any rate is to be treated not as matter for legitimate argument but as outrageous: a hurt not only to the believer but to his or her god. Faced with such towering objections, the free thinker sometimes wilts. Hardly realising it, he or she begins to share the ground trodden by religious zealots: that is, he or she begins tacitly to accept that there must be something wrong – so wrong, perhaps, that it should be stopped – in the making of attacks on religious faith that are so vigorous, so scornful, they excite such furious opposition.

But it will not do. Fury or no fury, the truth that the value of free expression, at least as a societal virtue, is morally prior to the content of anyone's beliefs applies as surely where the belief is religious as where it is political. The right of the believer to express his or her belief is no bigger than the right of the unbeliever to attack it. The violence of the believer's objection to the assault on his or her belief cannot conceivably justify its being proof against assault. That way lies nothing but the appeasement of extremism. A claim that the belief is true cannot justify a right in the believer not to have his or her belief attacked. That way lies nothing but a rule that the loudest voice prevails. A supposed justification based on a claim that the belief is *sacred* is even more dangerous. That way puts unreason on an unassailable throne. There is no escape from the necessity that critics and supporters meet on equal terms.

i. *The* McFarlane *Case*

The power of religious zealotry, or the fear of offending the zealots, is in the end an attack on the Rule of Law itself. The challenge that religious zealotry can pose to the law's integrity is I think illustrated by a case in the field of employment law: *McFarlane v Relate Avon Ltd.*[35] Mr McFarlane was dismissed from his employment with Relate as a counsellor because he refused to undertake psycho-sexual therapy with same-sex couples, though he had earlier said he would do so. He believed as a

---

[35] *McFarlane v Relate Avon Ltd* [2010] EWCA Civ 880.

Christian that same-sex sexual activity was sinful and that he should do nothing to endorse it. His claim of religious discrimination was dismissed in the Employment Appeal Tribunal, relying on its earlier decision in *London Borough of Islington v Ladele*[36] in which a registrar objected on religious grounds to gay marriage and was disciplined by her local authority employer for refusing to conduct civil partnership ceremonies. An application for permission to appeal to the Court of Appeal came before me in April 2010. I dismissed it.

I was particularly troubled by a witness statement made in support of the application by Lord Carey of Clifton, the former Archbishop of Canterbury. Among other things he said this:

> 20. ... I appeal to the Lord Chief Justice to establish a specialist Panel of Judges designated to hear cases engaging religious rights. Such Judges should have a proven sensitivity and understanding of religious issues and I would be supportive of Judges of all faiths and denominations being allocated to such a Panel. The Judges engaged in the cases listed above should recuse themselves from further adjudication on such matters as they have made clear their lack of knowledge about the Christian faith.[37]

This was a plea for a special court, together with a claim that judges who had participated in certain decisions of which Lord Carey disapproved ('the cases listed above') should recuse themselves from future litigation concerning what he called religious rights. Of Lord Carey's plea for a special court I said, 'I am sorry that he finds it possible to suggest a procedure that would, in my judgment, be deeply inimical to the public interest'.[38]

There were other points in the *McFarlane* case, prompted by Lord Carey's witness statement and the submissions of counsel for Mr McFarlane. I observed:

> The promulgation of law for the protection of a position held purely on religious grounds cannot therefore be justified; it is irrational, as preferring the subjective over the objective, but it is also divisive, capricious and arbitrary. We do not live in a society where all the people share uniform religious beliefs. The precepts of any one religion, any belief system, cannot, by force of their religious origins, sound any louder in the general law than the precepts of any other. If they did, those out in the cold would be less than citizens and our constitution would be on the way to a theocracy, which is of necessity autocratic. The law of a theocracy is dictated without option to the people, not made by their judges and governments. The individual conscience is free to accept such dictated law, but the State, if its people are to be free, has the burdensome duty of thinking for itself.[39]

For present purposes, however, I am principally concerned with Lord Carey's plea for a special court. I said it was 'deeply inimical to the public interest'; I think

---

[36] *London Borough of Islington v Ladele* [2009] ICR 387. Ms Ladele's appeal to the Court of Appeal was dismissed: [2010] IRLR 211. Both applied to the European Court of Human Rights, which refused their applications.
[37] *McFarlane* (n 35) [17].
[38] ibid [24].
[39] ibid [22].

that was an understatement. It was in reality a plea for a biased court, or at least a distinctly sympathetic one. Such a suggestion is not merely inimical to the public interest. It is contemptuous of the Rule of Law. Can you imagine it being suggested that the Lord Chief Justice should establish a specialist Panel of Judges designated to hear cases engaging political rights?

I am not concerned to dispute religious claims; far from it. If I were, it would have no proper relevance to this book. But as I have said, *McFarlane* illustrates the challenge that religious zealotry can pose to the law's integrity. It was not a free speech case; but free speech – and therefore, as I have argued, the Rule of Law – is especially vulnerable to zealotry in general and religious zealotry in particular. If you think you own a monopoly of the truth, you are liable to lose patience with those who disagree with you; liable, even, to suppose that they should not be allowed to disagree with you. But the notion of a single exclusive truth takes wing only as an article of faith, secular or religious. It cannot be translated into a recipe for government save at the price of tyranny and therefore brutality. Treated as an article of faith it offers, moreover, a spurious justification for suppression and arbitrary rule: a ruler who claims a monopoly of wisdom necessarily aspires to tyranny, because by definition he or she is always right.

There are degrees of these things. We are under no threat of tyranny in this jurisdiction. But every denial of free speech save on established objective grounds draws the blood of reason, fairness and the presumption of liberty: of the constitutional balance.

I would add a footnote. Nothing I have said is intended to suggest that individuals owe no duty to restrain their exercise of the right of free expression. Such an individual duty is owed every day, countless times a day, in the name of kindness and good manners. Good manners, I think, is the most unsung of all the virtues.

INDEX

Lightning Source UK Ltd.
Milton Keynes UK
UKHW020208080521
383339UK00003B/50